Helen Kostick

Come 'n' Get It!

Come 'n' Get It!

Recipes from Helen Kostick's Kitchen

MACMILLAN CANADA
TORONTO

Canadian Cataloguing in Publication Data
Kostick, Helen
Come 'n' get it!

Includes index.
ISBN 0-7715-7595-5
1. Cookery. I. Title.

TX715.6.K67 1999 641.5 C98-932511-3

This book is available at special discounts for bulk purchases by your group or organization for sales promotions, premiums, fundraising and seminars. For details, contact: Macmillan Canada, Special Sales Department, 29 Birch Avenue, Toronto, ON M4V 1E2. Tel: 416-963-8830.

Cover and interior design: Sharon Foster Design
Front cover photograph, pages i, v, and 182: Tim Leyes
All other photographs: Helen Kostick

We acknowledge the financial support of the Government of Canada through the Book Publishing Industry Development Program for our publishing activities.

Macmillan Canada
A Division of Canada Publishing Corporation
Toronto, Ontario, Canada
1 2 3 4 5 TRI 03 02 01 00 99
Printed in Canada

I would like to dedicate this book to my late husband Ed,
who was my biggest fan when it came to food.
Also, to my children Ken, Diane, Perry and Bobby,
as well as to my other foster children and all the
kids on the street who enjoyed my cooking.

And to my dear sister Phyllis.

Thank you all, I love you.

Acknowledgements

I would like to thank the following, all of whom helped make this book possible.

The City of Winnipeg—this is the greatest place in the world to live.

Macmillan Canada—Nicole, thank you for your wonderful laughter and making this book so enjoyable to do.

The Winnipeg Police Force (District 3)—all of you guys who visit me daily and who've sampled the recipes in this book: Andy, Dave, Keith, Raj, Pete, Al, Tony, Mark, Jason, Steve, Shannon, and everyone else. You bring a lot of joy to my life. Thank you.

Sokol Bingo Hall—all my bingo friends.

The Kwong family—my precious neighbours Mrs. Kwong, Channing, Corey and Jerry, who are like my own family. Thank you for being there for me.

Ken—my son, who helped make this book possible.

Jamie—who helped me look good on the cover and in the other pictures.

Georgette—my dear friend, who is always excited about my food and eager to do the dishes as long as she gets to sample.

Everyone who contributed recipes in this book.

Joe Skwarek—a true friend to our family who always enjoyed sampling my food, especially the pastries. Thank you for being a friend.

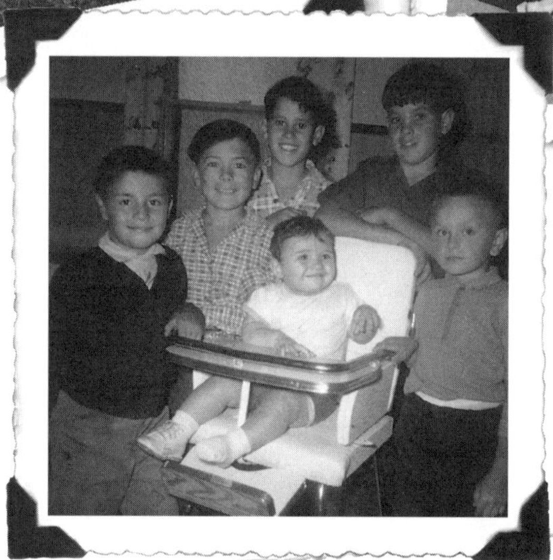

CONTENTS

Overleaf: A happy family.

Just Between Us

Well, you know, I've been cooking this "real" food for many years. As a wife and mother and foster mother, I was sometimes feeding as many as 9 people at a sitting. The kitchen became the family room, and cooking the most important family activity. I always tried to make the food I fed my family a little bit more interesting than the standard fare. Boy, did I create some wild recipes! Luckily, everyone seemed to enjoy them; I only had to force feed them occasionally (just kidding!). My husband, Ed, loved desserts so I learned to make pastries from scratch. It was all a labour of love; nothing gave me more enjoyment than watching Ed and the kids wolf down their food.

Even though money was scarce, we somehow always had more than enough (leftovers were a daily occurrence) so we made sure that not only friends and neighbours benefitted from the spill-over, but also our street friends. Over the years, as my neighbourhood grew and became more ethnically diverse, I've had the opportunity to learn to cook more exotic cuisine like Indian and Asian, as well as from numerous other nationalities.

Speaking of which, let me tell you about my own background. My father immigrated from England as a young man (and he was a lucky man, too, because he was to have travelled on the *Titanic* but missed the boat). I grew up on a farm in eastern Saskatchewan in the '30s and '40s (you notice I don't give exact dates!). Although I was motherless from the age of two, my family consisted of my father, sisters Florence and Phyllis, and my brother Alfred. Only Phyllis and I survive today.

My husband Ed Kostick, who was tall, dark and extremely handsome, was raised in a Ukrainian household and was used to eating Ukrainian food. After we met, I quickly learned how to cook specific Eastern European dishes, like perogies, adding my own special touches and thereby winning his heart.

Ed was a wonderful cook who often prepared meals for us (besides our foster children, Ed and I had two children, Ken and Diane). My son Ken also became a cook and at the age of five was preparing some interesting concoctions like fried wieners and scrambled eggs with ketchup and very thin pancakes (which I guess you could call crepes).

Inside this book is a collection of recipes from all those years, reflecting the many influences in my life but also the need to make delicious, sometimes interesting, meals on a small budget. I hope you enjoy these recipes and share the food with someone you love, as I have for many—so many—years.

Enjoy!

Helen Kostick

A Peek in Helen's Cupboard

In many of the following recipes, you'll catch a glimpse of what's in my cupboard—and in my fridge. In case there's anything you've never heard of, or if there's any uncertainty about what kind of butter I'm using, for instance, the list below should set you right.

Breadcrumbs: I have at least two cartons of fine, dry breadcrumbs always on hand.

Butter: speaking of butter, well, I always use the salted kind, even in my pastry.

Cooking Wine: some of my recipes call for cooking wine; any wine will do, even the drinking kind.

Cornstarch: always make sure you have a box of this handy: I do. Many of the Asian dishes in the section titled I'm Wonton More, courtesy of my neighbour Mrs. Kwong, call for cornstarch as a thickener (the secret is to mix it with twice the amount of water before adding it to the pot or wok; I always indicate this. If it reads only "cornstarch" don't add the water).

Dressing: well, I refer to stuffing as dressing, but if I'm dealing with salads, that's another matter. I tend to use the bottled kind, but feel free to make your own.

Mayonnaise: many of my salads would be nothing with out this!

Oil: I always have a bottle of vegetable oil handy (my son favours olive oil). Use what you have.

Oyster Sauce: this is a must for some of my recipes. All the grocery chains across the country now carry bottled oyster sauce. It is usually stocked in the Asian section. Once opened, keep refrigerated.

Rice: rice isn't as much a staple in my household as potatoes, but it almost is. I cook with the plain, long-grain white rice variety.

Soy Sauce: the soy sauce on the shelf in my cupboard is Chinese, not Japanese (I've yet to try the low-sodium option).

White Pepper: many of my dishes call for white pepper. Be sure to have a bottle handy, although feel free to substitute if need be.

Soups Worth Savouring

Overleaf: Forever plaid!

Quick and Easy Tomato Soup

SERVES 8

This is a great soup to make when it's the end of tomato season and you have too many hanging around.

5 large ripe tomatoes, peeled
1/4 cup finely chopped onions
1/2 clove garlic, crushed
1 tsp butter
3-1/2 cups milk
3/4 tsp baking soda
1/4 tsp salt

Crush tomatoes with a knife and fork. In a large pot, sauté onions and garlic in butter for 2 to 3 minutes or until onions are translucent. Add the tomatoes and simmer for 10 minutes.

Place in a blender or food processor and blend until smooth. Return to pot and add the milk. Heat on medium; be careful not to boil. Stir in baking soda and salt and serve.

Cream of Tomato Soup

SERVES 6

Serve this to children and watch them grow! (Ken is proof . . . he loved this soup.)

1 19-oz can tomatoes
2 tbsp minced onion
2 tbsp minced celery
1 bay leaf
1 tsp salt
1/4 tsp ground cloves
1/4 cup butter
1/4 cup all-purpose flour
2 cups milk
1 tsp sugar

In a large pot, heat tomatoes, onion, celery, bay leaf, salt and cloves. Simmer for 4 minutes. Remove bay leaf; place tomato mixture in blender or food processor and blend until smooth.

In the same pot, melt butter; add flour and stir until smooth. Stir in milk, stirring until smooth. Cook, stirring, at a gentle boil for 3 minutes.

Gradually, stir in the tomato mixture, stirring until heated through. Stir in sugar and serve.

Cream of Corn Soup

SERVES 4 TO 6

In the Kostick household, soup was served daily; this was a popular choice.

1 onion, diced
2-1/2 tbsp butter
2 tbsp plus 1 tsp all-purpose flour
1-3/4 cups milk
3/4 tsp celery salt
3/4 tsp salt
Pinch of white pepper
1 15-oz can creamed corn

In a large soup pot, cook onion in butter for 2 to 3 minutes or until translucent. Stir in flour; cook, stirring, for 1 minute. Gradually add milk, stirring constantly. Add celery salt, salt, pepper and corn; heat thoroughly on medium-high (be careful not to boil). Serve immediately.

Miss Helen Swain, on the farm.

Helen's Cream of Broccoli Soup

SERVES 6

This really is a "comfort" soup.

3 cups chicken stock
1 cup chopped onions
4 cups chopped broccoli
2 small bay leaves
1 clove garlic, chopped
1 tsp dried thyme, crushed
2 cups chopped potatoes
1/4 cup butter
3 tbsp all-purpose flour
1 tsp salt
1/2 tsp white pepper
2 cups half-and-half cream

In a large saucepan, combine stock, onions, broccoli, potatoes, bay leaves, garlic and thyme. Bring to a boil, then reduce heat and simmer for about 10 minutes or until vegetables are soft. Place soup in blender or food processor and purée until smooth.

In same saucepan, melt the butter. Blend in flour, salt and pepper; cook, stirring, over low heat for 2 minutes. Add cream all at once; cook, whisking, until mixture thickens. Stir in broccoli mixture. Continue to cook and stir until soup is thoroughly heated.

Potato Cream Soup

SERVES 4 TO 6

This is a delicious, hearty soup—perfect for keeping us Winnipeggers warm.

4 large potatoes, cubed
1-1/2 large onions, chopped
6-1/2 cups water
1-1/4 tsp salt
2-1/2 tbsp butter
3/4 cup whipping cream

In a large soup pot, add the potatoes, two-thirds of the onions, water and salt. Bring to a boil and boil until potatoes are tender. Reduce heat to simmer.

In a small frying pan, melt butter. Add remaining onion and sauté for 2 to 3 minutes or until translucent; add to soup. Stir in cream and cook on medium-low for 15 minutes. Using an immersion blender, blend soup until smooth and creamy. Serve immediately.

Onion Soup with Cheese

SERVES 6 TO 8

I've always used shredded Cheddar cheese in this soup, but who's to say you can't use Parmesan, or mozzarella, or whatever your heart desires?

5-1/2 cups milk
1/4 tsp paprika
Pinch of salt
Pinch of white pepper
2-1/2 tbsp butter
2-1/2 cups thinly sliced onions
2-1/2 tbsp all-purpose flour
1-1/2 cups shredded Cheddar cheese

In a saucepan, heat milk with paprika, salt and pepper. Set aside.

In a large saucepan, melt butter. Add onions and sauté until golden brown. Stir in flour until blended. Gradually stir in hot milk until smooth; simmer soup, being careful not to boil, for 10 minutes. Sprinkle cheese on soup and stir until cheese is melted. Serve, with toast if you like, immediately.

Helen, Ed (on tricycle), Ken and a friend.

Helen's Macaroni and Chicken Soup

SERVES 6

I make this soup especially for Const. Andrew Tighe because he enjoys it so much—he sometimes shares it with his fellow officers at work.

6 cups chicken stock
1 clove garlic, minced
1 onion, chopped
1 carrot, chopped fine
2 stalks celery, chopped fine
2 bay leaves
1 14-oz can Italian stewed tomatoes
1 19-oz can crushed tomatoes
1-1/2 tsp dried basil
1 15-oz can creamed corn
2–3 cups cooked macaroni
2 cups cooked chicken pieces
2 tbsp dry chicken soup base
Salt and pepper

In a large soup pot, add the stock, garlic, onion, carrot, celery and bay leaves; bring to a boil. Reduce heat and simmer for 15 minutes. Add tomatoes, basil and creamed corn. Simmer for 20 minutes, then add the cooked macaroni, chicken and soup base, stirring occasionally until heated through. Remove bay leaves. Stir in salt and pepper to taste and serve with grated Cheddar or Parmesan cheese.

Hamburger Soup

SERVES 6

This soup is very hearty and good for growing children; my children loved it, and look how they turned out!

1-1/2 lb ground beef
1 cup chopped onions
1-1/2 cups chopped cabbage
1 cup diced carrots
1 cup diced celery
1 cup cubed potatoes
1/4 cup pearl barley
2 tsp salt
1 tsp brown Bouquit Sauce or Worcestershire sauce
1/4 tsp white pepper
1 bay leaf
Pinch of dried basil
4 cups water
1 28-oz can stewed tomatoes

In a large pot, cook meat on medium-high, stirring, until brown. Drain off fat. Add onions and cook, stirring, for 2 to 3 minutes or until onions are translucent. Add the cabbage, carrots, celery, potatoes, barley, salt, brown sauce, pepper, bay leaf, basil and water. Bring to a boil, reduce heat and simmer, covered, for 20 minutes. Add tomatoes and continue simmering, covered, for 10 minutes or until the vegetables are tender.

Beef Barley Soup

SERVES 6

This soup is like a meal: after a bowl of this there's not much room for anything else (except, maybe, a piece of my apple pie).

3 lb beef short ribs
3 tbsp vegetable oil
2 cups canned crushed tomatoes
2 onions, sliced
1-1/2 tsp salt
5-1/2 cups water
2 cups chopped carrots
1 cup chopped celery
1 cup chopped cabbage
3/4 cup pearl barley
1/4 cup chopped parsley

In a large Dutch oven or saucepan, brown the ribs in oil. Add tomatoes, onions, salt and water. Simmer, covered, for 1-1/2 hours. Add carrots, celery, cabbage, barley and parsley. Continue simmering, covered, for 45 minutes. Remove from heat.

Remove ribs and cut meat from bones; cut into small pieces. Skim fat from soup and return meat to pot. If necessary, add more water or tomatoes. Heat for a few minutes longer and serve.

A Couple of Salads—Don't Hold the Mayo!

Overleaf: Always a bridesmaid, never a bride—well, not in this photo anyway.

Everyday Lettuce Salad

SERVES 4

I call this Everyday Lettuce Salad only because I could eat it every day.

1 small head lettuce, chopped
2 green onions, chopped
1 medium tomato, chopped
1/2 cup chopped cucumber
2 hard-boiled eggs, sliced

DRESSING:
1/4–1/2 cup mayonnaise
1 tsp white vinegar
1 tsp cooking oil
1/2 tsp sugar
1/4 cup half-and-half cream
Salt and pepper to taste

In a large bowl, toss together lettuce, green onions, tomato and cucumber.

DRESSING:
In a small bowl, beat together mayonnaise, vinegar, oil, sugar and cream until smooth. Pour over the lettuce mixture, mix lightly and garnish with egg slices.

Egg Salad

SERVES 4 TO 6

I used to serve this to Kenny and the gang at lunch time—all my kids loved egg salad sandwiches.

6–8 eggs
5 green onions, chopped fine
2-1/2–3 tbsp mayonnaise
Pinch of salt
Pinch of white pepper

Cook the eggs in boiling water until hard, 12 to 15 minutes. Place in a bowl of cold water until cold. Remove shells, place in a medium bowl and mash well. Mix in green onions, mayonnaise, salt and pepper. Serve with bread.

Ken, baby Diane, and my foster kids.

Chicken Salad

SERVES 4 TO 6

Try this salad on lettuce or as a sandwich; it's delicious both ways.

4 cups cubed cooked chicken
1 cup finely chopped celery
Pinch of salt
1 cup mayonnaise
1 tsp lemon juice
Pinch of paprika (optional)

In a medium bowl, combine chicken, celery and salt. In a separate bowl, cream the mayonnaise with the lemon juice; add to the chicken mixture. Arrange on lettuce on individual plates or in salad bowls and sprinkle with paprika, if desired, or prepare as sandwiches.

Ham Salad

SERVES 4 TO 5

This recipe is a great way to use up leftover ham. I often made it as a light lunch on Sundays for my family.

3 cups chopped cooked ham
1/2 cup chopped celery
1/3 cup sliced green onions
3 tbsp (approx.) mayonnaise
3/4 cup chopped cucumber
1/2 cup chopped pineapple
1 tbsp chopped parsley

In a medium bowl, combine ham, celery, green onions and enough mayonnaise to moisten; mix lightly. Garnish with cucumber, pineapple and parsley. Serve on lettuce as a light lunch.

Macaroni and Tuna Salad

SERVES 4 TO 6

This salad is great to take on camping trips (assuming you have a good cooler, because of the mayonnaise)—that's what my children used to do.

4 cups cooked macaroni
1 cup chopped celery
2 4.7-oz cans tuna, drained
3 green onions, chopped
1/2 cup chopped green pepper
1/4 cup chopped red pepper
Pinch of salt and pepper
1-1/2 cups mayonnaise

In a large bowl, mix together the macaroni, celery, tuna, green onions, green and red peppers, salt and pepper. Add the mayonnaise a little at a time, mixing constantly, until the macaroni mixture is all moistened.

Corn Salad

SERVES 4 TO 6

My late husband always enjoyed this salad with roast pork, gravy and mashed potatoes.

1 10-oz pkg frozen corn
1 medium tomato, sliced
1-1/4 cups sliced celery
1/2 cup chopped green pepper
1/2 cup pitted black olives, sliced
1/3 cup sliced green onions
1/4–1/2 cup mayonnaise

Cook corn according to directions on package. Drain and rinse. In a salad bowl, add corn, tomato, celery, green pepper, black olives, green onions, and dressing. Mix well and serve.

Substitution: A 12-oz can of corn may be used instead of frozen corn, but don't cook the canned corn!

Cabbage Raisin Salad

SERVES 6

I made this salad when I had a lot of company. Everyone really enjoyed it.

4 cups finely shredded cabbage
3/4 cup raisins
2 tbsp sugar
2 tsp salt
4–5 tbsp thick, creamy salad dressing
1 tbsp white vinegar

In a large bowl, combine cabbage, raisins, sugar and salt; let sit for 1 hour to season. Drain off any liquid. Mix salad dressing and vinegar in a small bowl. Spoon over cabbage mixture and toss.

Mr. Entertainer (Ken always stood out in a crowd), with Grandpa Swain, Ken Bremner and Ken Comber.

Carrot and Raisin Salad

SERVES 4

There are only five ingredients in this salad! What could be easier, and more delicious?

2-1/2 cups grated carrots
1/2–3/4 cup raisins
1/4–1/2 cup salad dressing
1 tbsp milk
1/2 tsp lemon juice

In a medium bowl, toss together carrots and raisins. In a separate bowl, blend the salad dressing, milk and lemon juice; add to the carrots and raisins, toss well and serve.

Substitution: I tend to use bottled salad dressing, but make your own if you have the time.

Cucumber and Apple Salad with Cheddar Cheese

SERVES 6 TO 8

Cheddar cheese is an old standby, and a good one, but you could use any cheese in the fridge.

3 cups cucumber slices
3 cups chopped apples
1/2–3/4 cup creamy cucumber salad dressing
1 head lettuce
1/2–3/4 cup shredded Cheddar cheese

In a large bowl, combine cucumber, apples and dressing; mix lightly. Arrange lettuce leaves on a plate; spoon on salad mixture. Sprinkle with cheese and serve immediately.

Substitution: Replace sliced cucumber with sliced zucchini.

Fruit Salad

SERVES 6 TO 8

This is a truly delicious and healthful salad; if Kenny was preparing this, he'd probably use low-fat sour cream and yogurt—there's no accounting for taste!

1-1/2 cups sliced bananas
1-1/2 cups orange sections
1-1/2 cups pineapple chunks
1-1/2 cups chopped apples
1-1/2 cups chopped peaches
1-1/2 cups unsweetened shredded coconut
1 cup mayonnaise
1/2 cup sour cream

In a large bowl, combine bananas, oranges, pineapple, apples, peaches and coconut. In a separate bowl, mix mayonnaise and sour cream together; add to the fruit salad and toss lightly. Chill in the fridge for several hours or overnight before serving. Serve on a bed of lettuce.

My Perogies, and Then Some

Overleaf: Helping Ken ride his tricycle.

Helen's Perogie Dough

SERVES 4 TO 6

This dough is very easy to work with and when cooked it's still soft. Everyone who has sampled my perogies loves the dough! You can double this recipe if you want to make more.

2 cups (approx.) all-purpose flour
1/2 tsp salt
1 cup warm water
1/4 cup corn oil

STEP 1. In a large bowl, mix flour and salt; make a well in the middle and pour the water and oil into the well. Mix together and add more flour, 1/2 cup at a time, until dough is firm. On a lightly floured surface, knead dough until mixture does not stick to your hands. Cover tightly and let stand for 30 minutes in a warm place.

STEP 2. On a lightly floured surface, roll out dough to 1/4-inch thickness. Cut into 2-inch circles.

STEP 3. Spoon 1 tsp filling onto centre, fold over and press edges to seal.

STEP 4. Bring a large pot of water to a boil, and add 1 tbsp oil. Add perogies. Stir occasionally so perogies don't stick to the bottom. They will cook in 3 to 4 minutes. When the perogies rise to the top, pour in 1 cup cold water to stop the cooking. Remove perogies with a slotted spoon and serve with topping (for topping ideas, see page 37).

Perogies with Potato, Bacon, Onion and Cheddar Cheese Filling

SERVES 4 TO 6

This is my most popular perogie recipe—you might want to try this one first.

Helen's Perogie Dough (see page 33)

FILLING:
2-1/2 lb medium red potatoes, peeled and cut in half
2 onions, chopped
1/2–3/4 lb bacon, chopped
2 tbsp butter
6 oz mild or medium Cheddar cheese, shredded (about 1-1/2 cups)

Prepare Helen's Perogie Dough according to instructions (step 1 on page 33); set aside.

FILLING:
In a large pot of lightly salted water, boil the potatoes for 30 minutes or until well done; drain and mash until there are no lumps left—the potatoes *must* be smooth.

While the potatoes are boiling, in a large frying pan over medium heat, cook the onions and bacon together for approximately 5 to 8 minutes or until onions are translucent. Stir in butter; remove and set aside 1/2 cup for topping. Stir the remaining bacon mixture and the cheese into the potatoes and mix well. Chill filling for at least an hour.

When chilled, follow instructions for filling and cooking perogies (steps 2–4 on page 33). Top cooked perogies with reserved topping.

Sweet Potato, Onion, Cheddar Cheese and Cinnamon Perogies

SERVES 4 TO 6

This is one of Kenny's favourite perogies.

Helen's Perogie Dough (page 33)

FILLING:
3 large sweet potatoes, peeled and cut into chunks
3/4 cup shredded medium Cheddar cheese
1-1/4 tsp cinnamon
2 onions, chopped fine
2 tbsp oil

Prepare Helen's Perogie Dough according to instructions (step 1 on page 33); set aside.

FILLING:
In a large pot of lightly salted water, boil the sweet potatoes until tender, approximately 30 minutes. Drain and mash until smooth; mix in cheese and cinnamon.

In a frying pan, sauté onions with oil until translucent. Mix onions into potatoes and let filling cool.

When cool, follow instructions for filling and cooking perogies (steps 2–4 on page 33). Serve with sour cream.

Wine Sauerkraut, Bacon and Onion Perogies

SERVES 4 TO 6

My late husband could never quite decide which he preferred most: me or my sauerkraut perogies!

Helen's Perogie Dough (page 33)

FILLING:
3–4 cups bottled sauerkraut
1/2–3/4 lb bacon, chopped
2 onions, chopped
2 tbsp butter
1/2 tsp salt
1/2 tsp white pepper

Prepare Helen's Perogie Dough according to instructions (step 1 on page 33); set aside.

FILLING:
Wash the sauerkraut in cold water to remove some of the sourness. Drain and finely chop to make it easier to spoon onto the dough.

In a frying pan, cook bacon and onions together, stirring frequently, until onions are translucent and bacon is soft—be careful not to burn. When cooked, stir in butter and cook, stirring, for another 2 minutes. Remove from heat and mix into sauerkraut along with the salt and pepper.

Place in a baking dish and cook, covered, at 350°F for 20 minutes. (By putting filling into the oven you will get the flavour of bacon and onions through the sauerkraut.) Chill in refrigerator before making perogies.

When chilled, follow instructions for filling and cooking perogies (steps 2–4 on page 33). Serve with Onion, Bacon and Butter Topping (page 37) and sour cream.

Onion, Bacon and Butter Topping

SERVES 4 TO 6

I get a lot of pleasure watching my family and friends eating my perogies with this topping; they get a lot of pleasure eating my perogies.

2 lb bacon, chopped
3 large onions, chopped
1/2 cup butter

In a large frying pan, arrange bacon. Spread onions on top. Cook at medium heat, without stirring, 15 to 20 minutes or until the fat from the bacon comes through the onions on top. Mix the onions and bacon together and cook for another 15 minutes, stirring often so it won't burn. Stir in butter and simmer for approximately 8 minutes. Remove from heat and let cool before transferring it to containers. You can freeze the topping for another time or serve with perogies immediately.

The men in my life.

Mushroom and Onion Perogies

SERVES 4 TO 6

This mushroom perogie recipe is easy and very tasty. If you want to use fresh mushrooms instead of canned, that's fine, but don't start getting fancy and using shiitakes or Portobellos! Buttons are the way to go.

Helen's Perogie Dough (page 33)

FILLING:
2 onions, chopped fine
2 tsp butter
3 10-oz cans mushrooms, drained and chopped
Salt and pepper to taste
1/2 cup mashed potatoes (optional)

Prepare Helen's Perogie Dough according to instructions (step 1 on page 33); set aside.

FILLING:
In a frying pan on medium heat, cook onions in butter for approximately 5 minutes, stirring often so they won't burn. Stir in mushrooms and cook for 5 to 8 minutes; stir in salt and pepper. Remove from heat and let cool.

When cool, follow instructions for filling and cooking perogies (steps 2–4 on page 33). If you find the filling slippery and it makes the dough edges too difficult to pinch together, add 1/2 cup of mashed potatoes to the filling.

Meat Loaf with Perogies

SERVES 6

I surprised my family with this one day—and they've never looked back.

1/2 lb ground pork
1/2 lb lean ground beef
1-1/2 cups instant mashed potato mix
1 onion, grated
1/2 cup fine dry breadcrumbs
1/2 tsp garlic powder
1/2 tsp dried basil
1/2 tsp salt
1/2 tsp pepper
2 eggs, lightly beaten
6 to 8 partly thawed frozen perogies

In a large bowl, mix together all the ingredients except the perogies. Place mixture in an 8- x 5-inch loaf pan. Take one perogie at a time and push it down into the meat, covering the holes so the perogies don't show through. Bake at 350°F for 45 minutes to 1 hour or until the meat loaf is done.

Let sit for 5 minutes before slicing.

Blueberry Perogies

SERVES 4 TO 6

Whenever my father-in-law came to visit, I'd whip up these. Naturally, we got along real well.

Helen's Perogie Dough (page 33)

FILLING:
2 tbsp sugar
1 heaping tbsp all-purpose flour
2 cups fresh or frozen blueberries

Prepare, roll out and cut Helen's Perogie Dough according to instructions (steps 1 and 2 on page 33).

FILLING:
In a medium bowl, mix together sugar and flour. Add blueberries, stirring so the berries are well coated.

Follow instructions for filling and cooking perogies (steps 3 and 4 on page 33).

Substitution: Cherries can be used (without the sugar and flour); so can prunes, plums, apples or any kind of fruit you want.

Cabbage Rolls, Casseroles and Other Favourites

Overleaf: My father in 1916, with Silver, Charlie, Dorky and Beauty.

Cabbage Rolls

SERVES 6

My family enjoyed this recipe whenever I made it, which was often and always at Christmas. You can always replace the bacon with ground meat —do try both, they're great.

2 heads cabbage
4 cups rice
1/2 lb bacon, chopped
2 onions, chopped
1/2 cup finely chopped celery
1 10-oz can tomato soup
Salt and white pepper
3 cups tomato soup
Pork fat or bacon (optional)

In a deep saucepan, steam the cabbage heads, one at a time, until the leaves are slightly soft and easy to peel. Peel off one leaf at a time and set aside; discard hard centre.

In a medium saucepan, add the rice, cover with water, bring to a boil and stir. Reduce heat, cover and let rice absorb all the water; the rice should only be partly cooked. Drain and set aside.

In a frying pan, cook the bacon, onions and celery until the celery is almost tender and the bacon is cooked but not crisp. Mix in rice, can of tomato soup and salt and pepper to taste. In a baking dish, place on the bottom any ripped cabbage leaves that are too difficult to roll. Using a whole leaf, spoon 1 tbsp of the mixture onto the centre, fold in each end and roll; place seam-side down in dish. Continue rolling and placing in layers to fill dish.

If you wish, top with pork fat or bacon. Pour tomato soup over.

Bake, covered, at 350°F for 2 hours or until the cabbage is cooked well and the rice is done. Serve hot.

Substitution: Stewed crushed tomatoes can be used instead of tomato soup.

Special Cabbage and Garlic Sausage

SERVES 6

I often experiment in the kitchen and am never certain what the results will be. This, however, was one very successful experiment!

2 tbsp lard
1 head cabbage, sliced
3 onions, chopped
1 large ring coarse garlic sausage, sliced
1/2 tsp salt
1/2 tsp white pepper

In a large frying pan, melt the lard over medium heat; cook cabbage and onions, stirring often, until cabbage is a little soft.

Remove from pan and place in a large baking dish. Stir in garlic sausage, salt and pepper; cook at 350°F for 25 to 30 minutes, stirring 2 or 3 times. Serve with mashed potatoes.

TIP: You can add green peppers or more garlic sausage, if you like.

Kostick Koleslaw

SERVES 6 TO 8

This recipe is a real family favourite, and it's a favourite with everyone else too.

1 head cabbage, shredded fine
2 large carrots, shredded fine
1/2 onion, shredded fine
1/2–3/4 cup mayonnaise
2 tbsp vegetable oil
1 tbsp white vinegar
1-1/2 tsp sugar
1/4 cup half-and-half cream

In a large bowl, combine the cabbage, carrots and onion; mix well. In a medium bowl, combine the mayonnaise, vegetable oil, vinegar, sugar and cream; blend until smooth. Pour mixture over vegetables and mix well. Let sit for 15 minutes. Before serving, mix again.

Borscht

SERVES 6

This is a traditional family meal that I continue to make for a few of my grown foster children—I just freeze what's left over for when they drop in.

4 lb pork spareribs
2 cloves garlic, chopped
20 cups water
2 onions, chopped
1 19-oz can stewed tomatoes
2 large carrots, shredded
2 cups shredded cabbage
1 cup chopped fresh spinach OR frozen
2 tsp dried dill
2 tsp salt
1/2 tsp pepper
4 medium beets, peeled and shredded
1 stalk celery, chopped fine
3 peeled and cubed potatoes
1/4 cup lemon juice

In a very large soup pot, add the ribs, garlic and water; bring to a boil. Boil until the meat is starting to fall off the bone; skim fat off the top.

Remove ribs and set aside. To the pot add onions, tomatoes, carrots, cabbage, spinach, dill, salt and pepper. Boil for 10 minutes, then stir in the beets and celery. Bring to a boil; reduce heat and simmer until the vegetables are soft. Meanwhile, remove meat from bones. Add meat and potatoes to pot; simmer until potatoes are done. Add lemon juice. If too sour, add a little sugar; if too sweet, add a little more lemon juice.

Serve hot with table cream or sour cream, whichever you prefer.

Stuff It! (in your bird)

MAKES 6 CUPS

This is a delicious everyday stuffing for chicken. Don't be afraid to add more poultry seasoning if you want. At Christmas, just double the recipe for a turkey.

1 large onion, chopped
2 tbsp butter
1 clove garlic, crushed
1 loaf sliced white bread, cubed
2-1/2 tbsp poultry seasoning
1/2 tsp white pepper
1/2 tsp salt
1 egg, beaten
3/4 cup milk

In a small saucepan, combine onion and 1-1/2 cups water. Bring to a boil and boil onion for 10 minutes, or until soft; drain. In the same saucepan, add butter and onion and return to heat; add garlic and sauté for another 3 to 4 minutes.

In a large bowl, mix together the bread, poultry seasoning, pepper and salt. Add onion mixture and mix well again. Pour in the egg and milk and mix with your hands. The mixture should be soft and easy to stuff into your chicken or turkey.

Chinese Noodles with Bacon

SERVES 4 TO 6

With the help of my neighbour Mrs. Kwong, and her daughter Channing, I've been able to master this dish.

1 pkg (1.1 lb) rice vermicelli noodles
3 eggs
2 large carrots, sliced into thin strips
1-1/2 lb bacon, chopped
2 cloves garlic, minced
3 onions, sliced
1 green pepper, sliced into strips
2 lb bean sprouts
1/4 cup soy sauce
2 tbsp oyster sauce
Salt and pepper
3 green onions, chopped

In a large bowl, soak the noodles in cold water until soft and fluffy, about 30 minutes; drain.

In a medium bowl, beat the eggs; pour into a heated, greased frying pan. Fry eggs until set on the bottom; turn and fry until cooked thoroughly. Remove and let cool; slice into small strips.

In a large wok bring 1/2 cup water to a boil. Place carrots in a steamer in the wok and steam, covered, for 3 to 4 minutes or until tender; remove carrots from wok and discard water.

Place the bacon in the wok and cook until almost crispy. Reduce heat and mix in garlic, onions, green pepper and bean sprouts, stir-frying for 4 minutes or until onions are translucent. Mix in noodles, soy sauce, oyster sauce, carrots and eggs; continue stir-frying until heated through. Add salt and pepper to taste.

Spoon stir-fry into a platter or large bowl and top with green onions. Serve immediately.

T-Bone Steak Marinated in Soy Sauce, Garlic, Honey and Beer

SERVES 6 TO 8

This was my late husband and my daughter's favourite.

1/2 cup mushroom soy sauce
2 tbsp liquid honey
3 cloves garlic, chopped fine
1 cup beer
3 T-bone steaks, 1/2-inch thick

In a large flat dish, combine soy sauce, honey, garlic and beer. Remove 1/2 cup and set aside to brush on steaks while cooking. Place the steaks in the marinade and turn to coat both sides. Let marinate, covered and refrigerated, for 1-1/2 hours, turning occasionally.

Place steaks on a hot grill and brush with the reserved marinade. Cook to desired doneness, brushing with reserved marinade.

Diane and Ed Kostick: in the 1960s.

Andy's "Hot" Chili

SERVES 8

Andy's chili is so delicious I had to share this recipe with you. You should know, by the way, that Andy is not only a great chili maker—he's also one of Winnipeg's finest constables.

2 tbsp vegetable oil
2-1/2–3 lb lean ground beef
4 cloves garlic, chopped
3 onions, chopped
4 stalks celery, chopped
2 green peppers, chopped
2 14-oz cans Italian stewed tomatoes with basil, oregano and garlic
2 10-oz cans tomato soup
1 19-oz can red kidney beans with water
2 10-oz cans sliced mushrooms, drained
2-1/2 tbsp white vinegar
1 tbsp chili powder
2 tsp salt
1 tsp pepper
1-1/2 tsp cayenne

In a large frying pan, heat the oil. Add the ground beef, half the garlic and half the onions; cook until the meat is no longer pink inside. Mix in celery, green peppers, tomatoes, tomato soup, beans, mushrooms, vinegar, chili powder, the remaining garlic, salt, pepper and cayenne. Bring to a boil. Let boil for 8 to 10 minutes, stirring often so nothing burns. Reduce heat and simmer for 1 to 1-1/2 hours, stirring often. If it isn't spicy enough, add a few drops of Tabasco sauce.

Substitution: If you don't have tomato soup, leave it out but use a 19-oz can of plain stewed tomatoes.

Constable Andrew Tighe, one of Winnipeg's very finest.

Spaghetti Sauce, Made with Garlic Sausage

SERVES 5

This is a different but tasty sauce. Serve it with spaghetti or other types of pasta.

1-1/2 large rings garlic sausage
1 tsp butter
1 onion, chopped
1 clove garlic, chopped
1/2 cup chopped celery
1 green pepper, chopped
1 19-oz can stewed tomatoes
1 10-oz can tomato soup
1 tsp chili powder
1/2 tsp cayenne

Skin the garlic sausage and put through a meat grinder or use a Handy Chopper; set aside.

In a large frying pan, heat the butter. Add onion and sauté for 3 minutes. Add the garlic, celery and green pepper; cook for 3 minutes. Add the ground sausage and cook for another 2 minutes. Stir in the tomatoes, tomato soup, chili powder and cayenne; simmer for approximately 30 minutes, stirring often. If you prefer it hotter, add Tabasco sauce. Serve over hot cooked noodles.

Rigatoni with Chicken

SERVES 6

My friend Georgette wants me to make this all the time. Now it's on paper, so make it yourself, Georgette! Good luck!

2 tbsp oil
1 onion, chopped
2 cloves garlic, chopped
1 stalk celery, chopped
1/2 cup chopped green pepper
1 14-oz can Italian stewed tomatoes
1 10-oz can golden mushroom soup
2 cups chicken stock
1/2 tsp dried basil
Salt and pepper
2 cups chopped poached chicken breasts
4-5 cups cooked rigatoni
1/2 cup grated Parmesan cheese

In a large frying pan, heat oil and sauté onion, garlic and celery for 5 minutes; mix in green pepper, tomatoes, mushroom soup, 1-1/2 cups chicken stock, basil and salt and pepper to taste. Simmer for 10 minutes.

Stir in cooked chicken and remaining 1/2 cup chicken stock and heat well before mixing in rigatoni and Parmesan. Serve immediately.

Old-Time Moose Soup

SERVES 6

This recipe is from Connie Morken, a good friend who lives down the street.

8 cups water
1-1/2 lb cubed boneless moose meat
Salt to taste
1/4 lb cubed pork
1 small onion, coarsely chopped
1/4 cup all-purpose flour
1/3 cup water

In a large soup pot, boil the water. Add the moose meat, and reduce heat; cover and simmer for 1 hour.

Add salt, pork and onion; cook for 10 to 15 minutes or until pork is tender.

In a small bowl, mix flour and water to form a smooth paste; stir into soup, boiling, until thickened.

Serve with Bannock (see page 55).

Substitution: If you can't find moose meat, replace with elk or beef.

Thanks for the Moose Soup, Connie.

Bannock

SERVES 6

You don't have to make Connie Morken's moose soup (see previous recipe) in order to enjoy her oven bread!

3 cups all-purpose flour
1 tsp salt
1 tbsp sugar
1 tsp baking powder
1/4 cup pan drippings OR lard at room temperature
2 cups cold water

In a large bowl, combine flour, salt, sugar and baking powder. With fork, stir in drippings or lard until evenly blended. Add water and mix to make dough; knead 10 to 12 times.

Turn out onto lightly floured board; roll or pat into circle about 1-1/2 inches thick. Bake on greased baking sheet at 375°F for 20 to 25 minutes or until golden.

Breakfast Prepared the Night Before

SERVES 6 TO 8

This great-tasting recipe, a variation of the X-mas Wife Saver, is from my bingo friend Mrs. Bernice Bilous.

12 slices bread
6 slices cooked turkey
5 slices salami
5 slices Cheddar cheese
5 slices mozzarella cheese
1/2 cup of canned mushrooms, drained
1/4 cup chopped spinach
1/2 small onion, coarsely chopped
1/4 cup chopped green pepper
3 tbsp tartar sauce
1/2 tsp salt
1/2 tsp white pepper
6 eggs
2 cups milk
2 cups finely crushed potato chips
1/2 cup butter

In a 9- x 13-inch pan, place a layer of bread; cover with all of the turkey and salami, then cheese, then another layer of bread.

In a food processor or with a Handy Chopper, process the mushrooms, spinach, onion, green pepper and tartar sauce until they are well chopped. Add salt and pepper to mixture.

In a medium bowl, beat eggs; stir in the milk. Add to spinach mixture and pour over bread. Cover and put in fridge overnight.

Top with crushed potato chips. Melt butter and pour over top. Bake at 350°F for 1 hour. Let sit for 10 minutes before serving.

Blueberry Pancakes

MAKES 1 DOZEN

This was Sunday breakfast in my house.

2 cups all-purpose flour
2 tbsp sugar
1 tsp baking soda
1 tsp salt
2 eggs, lightly beaten
2 tbsp vegetable oil
2 cups buttermilk
1-1/4 cups blueberries
6 tbsp lard (1 tbsp at a time for frying)

In a medium bowl, sift flour, sugar, baking soda and salt. Stir in eggs, oil and buttermilk just until flour is barely moistened. Gently fold in berries.

Using 1/4-cup measure, drop batter onto very hot, well-greased griddle or frying pan. Cook pancakes for approximately 3 minutes or until surface bubbles break; immediately turn over and cook second side for approximately 3 minutes or until golden brown.

Serve with butter and maple syrup.

Delicious Puffs with Whipped Cream

MAKES 1 DOZEN SMALL PUFFS

This is my favourite sister Phyllis MacDougall's specialty. Every time she comes to visit from Saskatchewan I strong-arm her into making some puffs.

1 cup water
1/2 cup salted butter
1 cup all-purpose flour
4 eggs
Whipped cream

In a saucepan, bring water and butter to a boil. Add flour all at once, beating vigorously with a wooden spoon, for approximately 2 minutes or until dough forms a smooth ball and cleans edges of pan. Remove from heat and let cool for a few minutes.

Add eggs, one at a time, beating thoroughly with a wooden spoon after each one. Drop by teaspoonfuls onto a greased cookie sheet and bake at 375°F for 35 minutes or until golden brown. Let cool on racks.

When cool, make a little slit in the top and fill with whipped cream.

Substitution: Any filling can be used instead of whipped cream.

There's Not a Lot of Seafood in Winnipeg, But . . .

Overleaf: The swinging Swain sisters (Helen, Phyllis and Florence).

Tuna Burgers

SERVES 6

A very special friend from bingo—Mrs. Edythe Cunningham—shared this recipe with me.

8 hard-boiled eggs, chopped
2 4.7-oz cans tuna, drained
3/4 cup mayonnaise
1/4 cup cream cheese, cubed
2 tbsp chopped green pepper
2 tbsp chopped onion
2 tbsp finely chopped sweet pickles
6 hamburger buns

In a large bowl, mix together the eggs, tuna, mayonnaise, cream cheese, green pepper, onion and sweet pickles. Form into patties and place on hamburger buns. Place the buns in a baking dish; cover with foil. Bake at 350°F for 4 minutes or long enough to thoroughly warm the buns. Serve immediately.

Tuna Casserole

SERVES 4 TO 6

This is another tasty and easy recipe from Edythe Cunningham.

1 4.7-oz can tuna, drained
1 10-oz can cream of mushroom soup
1/2 cup milk
2 cups cooked macaroni
1-1/2 cups crushed potato chips

In a medium bowl, mix together the tuna, soup, milk and macaroni. Place in a 1-1/2-quart casserole dish. Sprinkle with crushed potato chips. Bake at 350°F for 45 minutes.

Mickey (my childhood nickname) cuddling with a furry friend.

Shrimp Dish with Mushrooms

SERVES 4

I always make this recipe when company's coming!

3 tbsp butter
1 onion, chopped fine
1 small green pepper, chopped
1 clove garlic, chopped
1/4 cup minced pimento
1 cup rice
1/2 cup chopped mushrooms
1-1/2 cups cleaned shrimp
1 bay leaf
2 cups water
1 tsp salt

Melt the butter in a medium saucepan or frying pan on medium heat. Add onion, green pepper, garlic, pimento and rice; cook for 3 minutes or until onion is translucent. Stir in the mushrooms, shrimp, bay leaf, water and salt; cover. Once the water boils, reduce heat to low and simmer for 30 to 45 minutes or until rice is cooked. Remove bay leaf before serving.

Crabmeat Rolled in Bacon

SERVES 6

You'll thank me for this one at your next party!

1-1/2 cups flaked crabmeat
1-1/4 cups dry breadcrumbs
1/3 cup tomato juice
1 tbsp finely chopped onion
1-1/2 tsp chopped parsley
1/4 tsp dried basil
1/4 tsp salt
Pinch of white pepper
1 egg, lightly beaten
12 slices bacon

In a large bowl, combine the crabmeat, breadcrumbs, tomato juice, onion, parsley, basil, salt, pepper and egg; mix well. Shape into 12 finger-length rolls. Spiral each roll with a slice of bacon and secure with a toothpick. Place on a broiler rack and broil, turning frequently, until bacon is crispy.

Helen's Fish and Chips

SERVES 4 TO 6

fish and chips is nothing without beer.

2-1/2–3 lb haddock fillets
2-1/4 cups all-purpose flour
1 tbsp salt
1 tsp white pepper
2 large eggs
1 cup milk
3/4 cup beer
2 tbsp cooking oil
3–4 large potatoes

Cut each fillet into 4-inch pieces. In a medium bowl, sift the flour, salt and pepper. Coat the fillets in the flour mixture and set aside.

In another bowl, lightly beat eggs; stir in milk and beer. Add this mixture to the flour mixture; mix until smooth. (For thinner batter, use another 1/2 cup of milk.)

In a frying pan, heat oil. Dip the flour-coated fillet into the batter, then place in the hot oil. Cook until golden brown on both sides, turning once.

CHIPS:
Peel potatoes, slice lengthwise and then cut into strips.

In a deep-fryer, heat 6 cups oil on high; add potatoes and cook until golden brown. Drain, salt and serve.

Baked Fish Fillets

SERVES 6

This recipe is very easy and tastes great, or so my friends have told me. You can use cod, halibut, bluefish or whitefish—whatever strikes your fancy and isn't too oily.

1/2 cup milk
1 tsp salt
3/4 cup fine dry breadcrumbs
2 lb fish fillets (3 large fillets cut in half)
2 tbsp butter
1/2 cup grated Parmesan OR Cheddar cheese

In a large bowl, combine the milk and salt. Place the breadcrumbs in a separate large bowl.

Soak the fillets in the milk mixture for 3 to 4 minutes; drain, then roll in the breadcrumbs until each side is well coated.

Place fillets in a greased baking dish and dot with butter. Bake at 450°F for 20 to 30 minutes or until fish is cooked through. Sprinkle with cheese and bake for a minute or two before serving.

Creamed Pickerel Cheeks

SERVES 4

I love big fat fish cheeks; they're almost as yummy as fish thighs!

3 tbsp butter
1/2 cup finely chopped onion
1 lb jumbo pickerel cheeks
2 cloves garlic, chopped fine
1/4 tsp white pepper
1/4 tsp salt
1/4 tsp dried basil
1-1/2 cups whipping cream
1 tbsp cornstarch
1/4 cup milk
1 tbsp chopped chives

In a deep frying pan, heat butter. Add onion and sauté for 2 to 3 minutes or until translucent. Add the pickerel cheeks, garlic, pepper, salt and basil; cook for 6 to 8 minutes, stirring often. Add the cream and simmer for another 4 minutes.

In a small bowl, mix together cornstarch and milk. Add to the pan; stir until nice and creamy. Sprinkle in chives, stir and serve.

Baked Halibut with Peppers

SERVES 4 TO 5

This is a delicious, easy dinner.

1/4 cup melted butter
2 lb halibut, sliced
1/4 tsp salt
1/4 tsp white pepper
1/4 tsp dried basil
6–7 tomato slices
3/4 cup chopped green pepper
1/4 cup chopped red pepper
1/4 cup finely chopped onion

Pour the melted butter into a large baking pan. Place fish slices in one layer in pan and sprinkle with salt, pepper and basil. Top with tomato slices, green and red peppers and onion. Bake at 400°F for 25 to 30 minutes or until fish is cooked, basting occasionally with the melted butter and juices in the pan.

Ken on the Rouge (1968).

Pan-fried Spicy Sole

SERVES 4

I love fried breaded sole; serve this with a tossed salad and a cold soup.

4 large sole fillets, 1/2-inch thick
1 cup flour
2 tsp chili powder
1/2 tsp salt
1/2 tsp white pepper
2 eggs
1-1/2 cups fine breadcrumbs
1/4 cup vegetable oil

Cut the sole fillets in half. In a medium bowl, mix together the flour, chili powder, salt and pepper. In a separate bowl, beat eggs. Place breadcrumbs in a large bowl. Roll each fillet in the flour mixture, ensuring each side is well coated, then into the egg, and then into the breadcrumbs.

In a frying pan, heat the oil on high until hot but not smoking. Place the breaded fillets into the oil and brown each side, turning once; reduce heat to medium and cook for 10 to 12 minutes or until sole is cooked through.

Smoked Fillet Casserole

SERVES 2

You can replace the cod with any smoked fish.

2 pkg (about 4 oz each) pieces smoked cod
1/4 cup butter
2 tbsp chopped onion
1-1/2 tbsp chopped green pepper
1 tbsp chopped red pepper
1 tbsp chopped pimento
3-1/2 tbsp all-purpose flour
1-1/2 cups milk
1/4 tsp dried basil
1/4 tsp salt
Pinch of white pepper
1 1/4 cups breadcrumbs
1 tbsp melted butter
1 tbsp grated cheese

Place the fillets in a deep frying pan; cover with water and bring to a simmer; simmer gently until fish flakes easily when tested with a fork. Drain, cool and break into large flakes, removing any bits of bone.

In a large wok or frying pan, melt the butter; cook onion and green and red peppers until onion is translucent and peppers are tender. Stir in pimento. Push vegetables to one side of pan; add flour to pan juices and blend. Gradually add milk, stirring over medium heat until sauce thickens. Add flaked fish, basil, salt and pepper. Spoon into a greased 1-quart casserole dish.

In a small bowl, combine breadcrumbs, melted butter and cheese. Top fish with breadcrumb mixture and bake at 375°F for 15 to 20 minutes or until topping is browned and sauce bubbles.

Chicken and Turkey, Not Fowl

Overleaf: On the road with Kenny.

Breaded Chicken Steaks

SERVES 1 TO 2

A delicious accompaniment with these steaks is mashed potatoes with gravy: plain and simple!

1 large boneless chicken breast
1/2 cup all-purpose flour
Pinch of onion salt
Pinch of parsley flakes
Pinch of dried basil
Pinch of salt
Pinch of pepper
2 eggs
3/4 cup fine dry breadcrumbs
3 tbsp oil

Wash chicken and pat dry. Slice chicken in half lengthwise. Using a meat mallet, slightly flatten both pieces. In a pie plate, mix flour, onion salt, parsley, basil, salt and pepper. In a medium bowl, beat eggs. On another pie plate, spread the breadcrumbs. Coat the chicken in the flour. Dip into the eggs, then into the breadcrumbs, making sure both sides are well coated with crumbs. Heat oil on medium heat in a frying pan. Place the chicken in the pan and cook until bottom is browned; turn chicken and brown other side. Reduce heat and cook until chicken is no longer pink inside.

Substitution: Replace chicken with turkey.

Chicken Parmigiana

SERVES 6

This is Winnipeg Police Department Const. Keith Millen's recipe. As he said, "This is a simple and quick recipe—great for when you have people coming for dinner. My wife loves it!"

Marinara Sauce:
2 cloves garlic, minced
1 small onion, chopped
2 tbsp olive or salad oil
1 16-oz can tomatoes, crushed
1 5-oz can tomato paste
1 tbsp sugar
2 tsp dried basil
1-1/2 tsp salt

2 eggs
1 cup dry breadcrumbs
1 tsp salt
Pinch of pepper
6 chicken breasts
1 8-oz pkg mozzarella cheese, cut into 6 slices
1/4 cup grated Parmesan cheese

Marinara Sauce:
In a 2-quart saucepan over medium heat, cook the garlic and onion in oil approximately 5 minutes or until onion is translucent. Stir in tomatoes, their juice, tomato paste, sugar, basil and salt. Reduce heat to low, cover and simmer for 20 minutes or until thickened, stirring occasionally. You will need 2 cups of this marinara sauce.

In a pie plate, lightly beat eggs. Mix breadcrumbs, salt and pepper on waxed paper. Dip chicken in egg and then in breadcrumbs, coating thoroughly. Place breaded chicken breasts in greased 9- x 14-inch baking pan and bake at 350°F for 45 minutes. Spoon marinara sauce over chicken breasts and bake an additional 20 minutes. Top each breast with a slice of mozzarella, sprinkle with Parmesan cheese and cook until the cheese has melted. Serve immediately.

Kid on a car (1957).

Helen's Chicken Fingers

SERVES 2

This is a great snack, to be enjoyed with friends.

2 skinless, boneless chicken breasts
2 tbsp ketchup
1 tsp prepared mustard
1/2 cup all-purpose flour
Pinch of salt
Pinch of pepper
Pinch of garlic powder
Pinch of onion salt or powder
Pinch of basil
Pinch of parsley flakes
2 eggs
1 cup dry breadcrumbs
3 tbsp oil

Wash and pat dry the chicken; cut each breast into 4 strips. In a small bowl, mix together the ketchup and mustard. In a pie plate, mix together the flour, salt, pepper, garlic powder, onion salt, basil and parsley. In a shallow bowl, beat the eggs. In another pie plate, spread the breadcrumbs. Dip the chicken strips in the ketchup mixture, then into the flour, coating both sides. Dip into the eggs, then roll in the crumbs, coating both sides. In a frying pan with hot oil, brown chicken on both sides, then reduce the heat and cook until the chicken is white inside. Serve with sweet-and-sour sauce.

Substitution: Any other dipping sauce can be used.

Chicken with Peppers

SERVES 3 TO 4

I recommend this recipe because it's fast and tasty. Serve with plain rice.

2 skinless, boneless chicken breasts, cut into chunks
3/4 tsp salt
1/4 tsp pepper
1-1/2 tsp cornstarch
2 tbsp corn oil
1 green pepper, sliced
1/2 red pepper, sliced
1 8-oz can sliced mushrooms, drained
1 small onion, chopped fine

In a bowl, mix the chicken, salt, pepper and cornstarch. Heat oil in a saucepan over high heat. Add chicken and stir continuously until it turns white, approximately 15 minutes. Add peppers, mushrooms and onion; simmer for 5 minutes or until onions are translucent. If the chicken starts to stick to the pan, add about 2 tbsp chicken stock.

Chicken and Mushrooms with Cream

SERVES 3 TO 4

This is a great dish to make with leftover chicken or turkey. If you prefer a spicier dish, by all means add red and green peppers and other spices.

1 small onion, chopped fine
1/2 clove garlic, minced
2-1/2 tbsp butter
1-1/2 cups cubed cooked chicken
1 8-oz can mushrooms, drained and sliced
2-1/2 tbsp all-purpose flour
1-1/2 cups chicken stock
1/2 tsp salt
1/2 tsp pepper
1/4 tsp cayenne
Pinch of nutmeg
1 large egg
4 tsp cream

In a medium saucepan, sauté onion and garlic in 1/2 tbsp of the butter for 8 minutes. Add the rest of the butter, chicken and mushrooms; cook, stirring, for 5 minutes. Add the flour and mix well; stir in the chicken stock. Simmer for 10 to 12 minutes. Season with salt, pepper, cayenne and nutmeg. Beat the egg with the cream and stir into the chicken mixture. Cook for 2 more minutes and serve.

Substitution: Replace chicken with turkey.

Baked Chicken with Dressing

SERVES 4

A very good friend and neighbour, Nettie Rogowski, very kindly shared this recipe.

1/2 cup butter or margarine
1 cup chopped celery
1/2 cup chopped onion
1/2 cup shredded carrots
3–4 cups dry breadcrumbs
1-1/2 tsp dried sage
1 tsp pepper
1/2 tsp salt
2–3-lb chicken, cut into serving pieces

In a medium saucepan, melt butter. Sauté celery, onion, and carrots until onion is translucent; remove from heat. In a large bowl, mix together the breadcrumbs, sage, pepper and salt and the onion mixture; mix well. If necessary, add 1/2 cup water to moisten mixture. Place the chicken pieces in a small roasting pan. Put dressing mixture over top; do not pack. Bake at 350°F for 45 to 60 minutes or until chicken is cooked.

Oven-Baked Chicken and Rice

SERVES 4

This Kostick family favourite is fast, easy and very tasty.

1 small onion, chopped fine
1 clove garlic, crushed
1 tsp cooking oil
1 10-oz can condensed cream of mushroom soup
1-1/4 cups water
3/4 cup rice
1/2 tsp paprika
1/2 tsp parsley flakes
1/4 tsp salt
Pinch of pepper
4 chicken breasts

In a medium frying pan, sauté onion and garlic in oil until onion is softened. Add the mushroom soup, water, rice, paprika, parsley, salt and pepper; stir until smooth. Pour mixture into a 2-quart shallow casserole dish. Place chicken breasts on top of mixture. Sprinkle with a little more paprika and bake at 350°F for 45 to 55 minutes or until the chicken is no longer pink inside.

Diane and Ed Kostick in the 1980s.

Nettie's Chicken with Spanish Rice

SERVES 4

Once again, I'm grateful to my friend Nettie Rogowski for revealing the recipe for this dish. Sometimes I add chopped red and green peppers.

2 tbsp butter
2 onions, sliced
1-1/2 cups water
2 cloves garlic, crushed
1 28-oz can tomatoes, drained and chopped
1/2 tsp dried basil
1/2 tsp dried oregano
3/4 tsp salt
Pinch of pepper
1 cup rice
4 skinless chicken breasts, with bone in
3 tbsp grated Parmesan cheese

In a large saucepan, melt butter. Add onions and sauté until translucent. Add the water, garlic, tomatoes, basil, oregano, salt and pepper. Bring mixture to a boil. Pour into 2-1/2-quart casserole dish. Stir in rice; place chicken on top. Cover and bake at 350°F for 45 to 55 minutes or until chicken is cooked through. Sprinkle with Parmesan and broil for 2 to 3 minutes.

Helen's Chicken and Spinach Roll-ups

SERVES 4 TO 6

I'd like to set the record straight: I came before Ken and so did these roll-ups!

4 large skinless, boneless chicken breasts
1 tbsp cooking oil
1/2 tsp salt
1/2 tsp white pepper
1-1/2 cups chopped fresh spinach
8 slices mozzarella cheese
4 slices ham
1 small onion, sliced thin
1/4 tsp garlic powder
1/4 tsp paprika

Using a meat mallet, gently pound the chicken breasts to 1/4-inch thickness. Brush breasts with half of the oil; sprinkle with salt and pepper. Top each with about 1/3 cup of the spinach, a slice of cheese, a slice of ham, and a slice of onion. Roll up breasts and secure with a toothpick. Arrange in a small nonstick baking dish and brush with remaining oil. Sprinkle with garlic powder and paprika and top each with another slice of cheese. Bake at 375°F for 20 to 25 minutes or until the chicken is no longer pink inside. Slice and serve.

Helen's Chicken à la King

SERVES 6

This is a big hit with my family and neighbours, especially the Kwong family.

3 tbsp shortening
1 onion, chopped
1 clove garlic, chopped fine
1/2–1 cup chopped celery
1 cup shredded carrots
1 cup mushroom pieces or slices
2 tbsp dry chicken soup base
1/2 tsp dried basil
1/2 tsp parsley flakes
3 cups milk
4 cups bite-size cooked chicken
2 10-oz cans cream of chicken soup
1 cup frozen peas
3 tbsp all-purpose flour
Salt and pepper to taste

In a large saucepan, melt the shortening. Add onion, garlic, celery and carrots; cook gently for 10 minutes. Stir in mushrooms, chicken soup base, basil and parsley. Add the milk and continue to stir. Add the chicken, cream of chicken soup and peas. Cook on low heat for about 15 minutes or until the vegetables are cooked. Mix the flour with a little water and stir into the pot to thicken the chicken mixture. Add salt and pepper to taste.

Substitution: Turkey can be used instead of chicken.

Poached Chicken with Herbs

SERVES 4

I love this recipe—it always tastes great. (You might want to poach more at the same time to make chicken salad or chicken sandwiches.)

4 cups water
2 cloves garlic, crushed
3 tbsp dry minced onion
1 tsp dried basil
1 tsp parsley flakes
1/4 tsp oregano
1/4 tsp salt
1/4 tsp white pepper
1 bay leaf
4 skinless, boneless chicken breasts

In a deep frying pan, bring the water to a boil. Add garlic, minced onion, basil, parsley, oregano, salt, pepper and bay leaf. Reduce heat and simmer for approximately 10 minutes; add the chicken and poach 15 to 20 minutes or until meat is no longer pink inside. Remove chicken from pan. (I keep the broth to make soup.)

Roast Chicken

SERVES 6

With the leftover chicken from this recipe, try the Chicken Salad (page 23) or my Chicken à la King (page 83).

5–7-lb roasting chicken
2 cloves garlic, crushed
1/4 cup soft butter
1/2 tsp salt
1/2 tsp white pepper
Dressing (your recipe or mine, see page 47)

Wash chicken and pat dry; place in a small roasting pan. Mix the garlic with the butter. Using half of the butter mixture, rub the whole inside of the chicken and sprinkle half of the salt and pepper inside. Stuff with dressing and rub the rest of the butter over top. Sprinkle the remaining salt and pepper over the chicken. Roast at 350°F for 2-1/2 to 3 hours or until chicken is thoroughly cooked, basting the chicken often to keep it moist.

Substitution: A small turkey can be used instead of a roasting chicken.

Guess which one is Ken?

Chicken Stir-fry

SERVES 5 TO 6

Serve this stir-fry over steamed rice; it's delicious and filling.

1-1/2 skinless, boneless chicken breasts
4 tbsp soy sauce
1 tbsp cornstarch
1/2 tsp sugar
1-1/2 cloves garlic, minced
2 tbsp cornstarch
1/2 tsp hot red pepper flakes
1 cup water
2-1/2 tbsp cooking oil
2 carrots, sliced thin diagonally
1 onion, chopped
2 stalks celery, sliced thin diagonally
1/2 red pepper, sliced diagonally
1/2 green pepper, sliced diagonally

Slice chicken into thin strips. In a medium bowl, combine 1 tbsp of the soy sauce, 1 tbsp of the cornstarch, sugar and garlic; stir in the chicken and set aside. In another bowl, blend remaining cornstarch, remaining soy sauce, hot red pepper flakes and water; set aside. Heat 1 tbsp of the oil in wok or frying pan over high heat. Add chicken and stir-fry until tender; remove. Add remaining oil to the wok; stir-fry carrots, onion, celery and red and green peppers for 3 to 4 minutes. Stir in chicken and soy sauce mixture, stirring continuously, until sauce boils and thickens. Serve immediately over rice.

Chicken Stew

SERVES 6

Most people never think of stewing chicken; try this and you'll never look back.

1 frying chicken, cut into serving pieces
4-5 tbsp cooking oil
1 large onion, chopped
1-1/2 cups chopped carrots
1 cup chopped celery
2 cloves garlic, chopped
4–5 cups chicken stock
1 tsp dried basil
1 tsp parsley flakes
1 tsp salt
1 tsp pepper
1 cup peas
4 large potatoes, peeled and cubed

In a large deep ovenproof saucepan, brown the chicken in the oil. Remove chicken and set aside. In the same pan, sauté the onion. Mix in carrots, celery, garlic and 1/4 cup of the chicken stock, cook for 5 minutes. Return chicken to pan. Pour in rest of chicken stock; sprinkle in basil, parsley, salt and pepper. Bake at 350°F for approximately 30 minutes. Add the peas and potatoes and cook until the potatoes are cooked, approximately 20 minutes. If you prefer a thicker stew, just add 2 tbsp flour mixed with 1/2 cup water or chicken stock and stir. Serve hot.

Chicken Loaf

SERVES 6

This is another perfect dish for using up leftover chicken. Serve with a salad on the side.

3 eggs
2-1/2 cups dry breadcrumbs
1/2 cup finely chopped celery
2 tbsp chopped pimento
2 tbsp chopped green pepper
1 tbsp Worcestershire sauce
1 clove garlic, chopped fine
1 tsp salt
3 cups chicken, cubed
1/2 cup canned mushrooms, drained and chopped
1 10-oz condensed cream of mushroom soup
1 cup chicken stock

SAUCE:
3/4 cup sliced or chopped mushrooms
1 cup sour cream
1/2 tsp salt
Pinch of pepper

LOAF:
In a large bowl, combine eggs, breadcrumbs, celery, pimento, green pepper, Worcestershire sauce, garlic, salt, chicken pieces, mushrooms, mushroom soup and chicken broth; mix well. Place mixture in a 5- x 9-inch greased loaf pan and bake at 350°F for 40 minutes.

SAUCE:
In a small saucepan, mix together mushrooms, sour cream, salt and pepper; heat on medium for 20 minutes or until mushrooms are cooked. Pour over sliced chicken loaf. Serve immediately.

Chicken Pie

SERVES 4 TO 6

This easy pie recipe calls for only one pie shell and no upper crust.

1/2 cup chicken stock
1-1/2 cups diced cooked chicken
1/3 cup diced cooked celery
1/3 cup diced cooked potatoes
2 tbsp chopped parsley
1/4 tsp dried sage
1 tbsp butter
1 tbsp grated onion
1/2 cup boiling water
2 chicken bouillon cubes
1 cup milk
3 eggs
1/2 tsp salt
Pinch of pepper
1/4 tsp paprika
Pinch of nutmeg
1 deep 9-inch unbaked pie shell
1/2 cup shredded mozzarella cheese

In a medium pot, heat chicken stock. Add chicken, celery, potatoes, parsley and sage. Remove from heat and let cool. Melt butter in a medium saucepan and cook onion gently for 3 minutes. Add water and bring to a boil; stir in bouillon cubes until dissolved. Stir in milk and heat just to scalding point; remove from heat. In a bowl, beat eggs. Add salt, pepper, paprika and nutmeg; blend well. Add hot milk mixture gradually, beating gently. Spoon chicken mixture into pie shell. Pour milk mixture over chicken and sprinkle with cheese. Bake at 375°F for 35 to 40 minutes or until a knife inserted in the centre comes out clean. Let sit for 10 minutes before serving.

Roast Turkey Breast with Dressing

SERVES 2 TO 4

This is another of Ken's favourite recipes!

2 large skinless turkey breasts, with bone in
3 cloves garlic, minced
Dressing (your recipe or boxed kind)
1/4 cup butter
1/4 tsp salt
1/4 tsp pepper
1/2 cup water

Wash and pat dry the turkey. Make little slits in the top and insert some of the garlic. Stuff with dressing on the bone side and tie breast with kitchen string. Add the remaining garlic to the butter; rub over the turkey and sprinkle with salt and pepper. Place in a baking dish with water and cover. Bake at 350°F for 1 to 1-1/2 hours or until the turkey is completely cooked, basting 2 or 3 times to keep from drying out.

Helen's Beef!

Overleaf: Ken on a calf (1960).

Beef Pot Roast

SERVES 6

This Beef Pot Roast brings back fond memories of family dinners.

4–5-lb beef roast (chuck shoulder, rump or round)
1 large onion, sliced
2 cloves garlic, chopped
Salt and pepper to taste
1–2 cups water or tomato juice
6 carrots, chopped
6 potatoes, halved
1/2 cup chopped celery

In a heavy roasting pan, brown the roast slowly, adding a little cooking oil if there isn't enough fat on the roast. When browned, add the onion, garlic, salt and pepper. Add the water; cover and put it in the oven at 350°F for 1 hour. Add carrots, potatoes and celery; cook, covered, until the vegetables are tender, about another hour. (Make sure there is liquid in the pan at all times.) Slice roast and serve with the vegetables.

Beef Stew

SERVES 6

This stew is easy to make and probably very good for you. Experiment with flavourings.

2 lbs cubed stewing beef
2 onions, chopped
2 cloves garlic, chopped
1 beef bouillon cube
1 cup boiling water
1 tsp salt
1/2 tsp pepper
4 carrots, chopped
1 cup chopped celery
3 large potatoes, chopped
1/4 cup all-purpose flour

In a large frying pan on high heat, cook the beef with a little lard or shortening for approximately 3 minutes; reduce to medium heat. Add onions and garlic; cook until the meat is browned. Dissolve the beef cube in boiling water and pour over meat; sprinkle with salt and pepper. Transfer to a casserole dish. Stir in the carrots and celery. Bake at 300°F for 1 hour; add potatoes and bake for 15 minutes more. Mix the flour with 3 tbsp water. Stir into stew and cook for another 10 minutes.

Hamburger Steak

SERVES 8

My late husband used to make this on the weekends when it was his turn to cook. Be creative with the flavourings, as my husband was, and use garlic, basil, chili powder or whatever you like.

2 lb ground beef
2 eggs, lightly beaten
1/2 cup tomato juice
2 tsp prepared mustard
1 tsp salt
1/2 tsp pepper
1/2 cup dry breadcrumbs

In a large bowl, mix together the ground beef, eggs, tomato juice, mustard, salt, pepper and breadcrumbs; use your hands and shape into eight 2-1/2-inch-thick patties. Broil or fry patties until completely cooked. Serve with mashed potatoes, fried onions and mixed vegetables.

Helen's Hamburgers

SERVES 4 TO 6

I haven't had a complaint yet about this one.

2-1/2 lb ground beef
1 onion, chopped fine
1 clove garlic, minced
1 egg, beaten
2 tbsp ketchup
1 tbsp prepared mustard
1/2 tsp salt
1/2 tsp pepper
Hamburger buns

In a large bowl, mix together ground beef, onion, garlic, egg, ketchup, mustard, salt and pepper; use your hands to shape into 4 to 6 patties. Grill or fry patties for 10 to 12 minutes or until well done. Place on hamburger buns and top with your favourite toppings.

Helen's Sloppy Joes

SERVES 6

Whenever I took the trouble to ask the kids what they wanted for dinner, this was it.

1 lb ground beef
1 onion, chopped
1-1/4 cups finely chopped celery
1 clove garlic, chopped fine
1-1/2 cups beef stock
1-1/2 cups tomato sauce
1/2 tsp Worcestershire sauce
Salt and pepper to taste
Hamburger buns

In a large frying pan, combine beef, onion, celery and garlic. Cook, stirring frequently, until the beef begins to brown and the onions are tender. Drain fat and stir in stock, tomato sauce, Worcestershire sauce, salt and pepper. Heat until it starts to boil. Cook, constantly stirring, for 2 to 5 minutes longer. Toast hamburger buns, place on plates and top with sloppy joe mixture. Cover with the top half of the bun and serve.

Helen's Shepherd's Pie

SERVES 6 TO 8

This is one of the simplest and most creative ways to use leftovers—add whatever vegetables you have.

4-1/2 cups chopped leftover roast beef
3 cups leftover gravy
1-1/2 cups frozen peas
4-1/2–5 cups mashed potatoes
1 small egg, lightly beaten

In a buttered baking dish, place the beef, gravy and peas. Cover with the mashed potatoes, brush potatoes with the beaten egg, and bake at 350°F until the potatoes are slightly browned, about 45 minutes.

A housewife and mother in the 1950s

Helen's Dynamite Meat Loaf

SERVES 4

This meat loaf was always prepared when I had plenty of leftover vegetables. Try your own variation.

1 lb ground beef
1 small onion, chopped fine
2 eggs
1 cup dry breadcrumbs
2 tbsp prepared mustard
2 medium tomatoes, chopped
1 green pepper, chopped
1 tsp garlic powder
1 tsp chili powder
1/2 tsp black pepper
1/2 tsp salt

In a large mixing bowl, combine the ground beef, onion, eggs, breadcrumbs, mustard, tomatoes, green pepper, garlic powder, chili powder, black pepper and salt; mix well with your hands—have lots of fun! Shape the meat loaf to fit in a 5- x 9-inch loaf pan or casserole dish. Bake at 350°F for 1-1/2 hours. Allow to cool 5 minutes; cut into 1-inch slices and serve.

Substitution: Replace ground beef with ground pork, ground chicken or ground turkey.

Ground Beef Hash

SERVES 8 VERY HUNGRY CHILDREN

There isn't a child that won't like this dish, trust me.

1/2–1 cup macaroni
Pinch of salt
1-1/2 lbs ground beef
2 tbsp fat
2 onions, minced
1 clove garlic, minced
2 carrots, minced
1-1/2 cups canned tomatoes
Salt and pepper to taste

Cook macaroni in boiling water with a little salt until tender, then drain. In a large frying pan, brown ground beef in fat. Add onions and garlic; cook slightly. Mix in the carrots, tomatoes, salt, pepper and cooked macaroni. Turn into a greased baking dish and bake at 350°F for 30 minutes or until slightly browned.

Substitution: Lard or shortening can be substituted for the fat. Gravy can be substituted for the canned tomatoes.

Meat Balls and Gravy

SERVES 6

This was a big hit with the "little man" Ken and the friends he brought home after school.

MEAT BALLS:
3 lbs ground beef
1 large onion, chopped fine
2 cloves garlic, crushed
2 eggs, lightly beaten
1 cup fine dry breadcrumbs
Salt and pepper to taste

GRAVY:
4-1/2 cups water
1 OXO beef cube
3 tbsp all-purpose flour, mixed in 3/4 cup water
Salt and pepper to taste

In a large bowl, mix together with your hands the ground beef, onion, garlic, eggs, breadcrumbs, salt and pepper. Shape into balls (approx. 2 tsp for each) and place on waxed paper until all the balls are made. In a frying pan, brown the balls on every side. Transfer into a large casserole dish. In the same frying pan, bring the water to a boil. Add the beef cube and stir until dissolved. Add flour mixture, salt and pepper. Bring to a slow boil and cook, stirring until thickened; strain the gravy over the meatballs to get all the lumps out. Bake at 350°F for 45 minutes. Serve with mashed potatoes and vegetables or spaghetti.

Chili Con Corny

SERVES 4 TO 6

This dish really went over big with the Kwong brothers, Corey and Jerry.

2 tbsp fat or cooking oil
1-1/2 lb ground beef
1/2 green pepper, chopped
1 onion, chopped
1 clove garlic, chopped fine
2 cups canned kidney beans, rinsed
1 28-oz can tomatoes
1 12-oz can whole kernel corn
1-1/2 tsp chili powder
1/2 tsp salt
1/2 cup (approx.) water

Heat fat in a large frying pan and sauté beef, green pepper, onion and garlic until lightly browned, stirring frequently. Add beans, tomatoes, corn, chili powder and salt. Mix well and simmer for approximately 30 minutes, stirring occasionally. If mixture becomes too thick, gradually stir in the water. Serve hot with toast.

Chili with Noodles

SERVES 6 TO 8, DEPENDING ON THE SIZE OF YOUR GUESTS

I really enjoy this with a few drops of Tabasco sauce—but then, it's great with or without it!

1-1/2 lbs ground beef
1/4 cup fat
1 small onion, chopped fine
1/2 cup finely chopped celery
1 small clove garlic, crushed
2-1/2 tbsp all-purpose flour
2-1/2 cups stewed tomatoes
1 tsp salt
1/2 tsp chili powder
1-1/2 tsp Worcestershire sauce
1/2 cup water

Brown the beef in a saucepan with the fat. Remove the meat and set aside. Add onion, celery and garlic to the pan; blend in the flour. Add tomatoes and cook slowly until thickened, stirring constantly. Add salt, chili powder, Worcestershire sauce, ground beef and water. Cook for another 10 to 12 minutes, stirring occasionally. Serve on a bed of hot cooked noodles of your choice.

Substitution: The fat can be replaced with lard or shortening.

Noodles, Spinach and Beef Casserole

SERVES 6 TO 8

This recipe is so easy to make, it makes a great Sunday dinner.

4 cups broad egg noodles
2 10-oz pkg frozen spinach
1-1/2 lb ground beef
1/2 cup fine dry breadcrumbs
1 egg, lightly beaten
1/4 tsp nutmeg
1/2 cup grated Parmesan cheese
3/4 cup finely chopped onion
1/4 cup margarine
1/2 cup all-purpose flour
1 tsp salt
1/4 tsp pepper
Pinch of dried oregano
Pinch of nutmeg
2 cups chicken stock
2 cups milk
Dash of hot sauce
2 egg yolks

Cook noodles in boiling salted water for 7 to 10 minutes or until tender; drain and set aside. Cook and drain spinach; set aside. In a large frying pan, brown the beef; drain fat. Add the spinach, breadcrumbs, egg, 1/4 tsp nutmeg and cheese; stir well and set aside. In a saucepan, sauté onion in margarine until translucent. Stir in flour, salt, pepper, oregano and a pinch of nutmeg; cook, stirring, for 1 minute. Slowly stir in broth and milk and heat, stirring, until sauce boils. Remove from heat. Blend hot sauce into the egg yolks and stir into the sauce. In a shallow 3-quart baking dish, alternate layers of sauce, noodles and meat, ending with sauce. Top with more cheese if desired. Bake at 375°F for 25 minutes or until sauce is bubbling.

Ken and his foster sister, Cindy, in 1964.

Beef and Macaroni Casserole

SERVES ABOUT 6

All my children (the foster ones too) loved this dish so much that I had to double the recipe every time—they always had seconds.

1-1/2 lb ground beef
3 cloves garlic, minced
2 onions, chopped
1 5-oz can tomato paste
2-1/2 tbsp Worcestershire sauce
1-1/2 tsp dried basil
3/4 cup mayonnaise
1/2 cup all-purpose flour
2-1/4 cups milk
3 eggs, beaten
6–8 cups cooked macaroni
3 cups shredded mozzarella cheese
1 cup grated Parmesan cheese

In a deep frying pan, brown the beef with garlic and onions. Stir in tomato paste, Worcestershire sauce and basil; simmer for 5 minutes. In a saucepan over low heat, combine the mayonnaise and flour. Gradually stir in the milk, cooking gently, until thickened. Stir in eggs and cook, stirring, for another 3 minutes. Remove from heat, and stir in the macaroni and half of the mozzarella cheese. In a 12- x 8-inch casserole dish, layer half the macaroni mixture; spread all the meat sauce on; spread on the remaining macaroni mixture. Top with the remaining mozzarella and Parmesan cheese. Bake, covered, at 350°F for 25 minutes. Uncover and bake 10 to 15 minutes longer to brown.

Liver and Onions

SERVES 4 TO 6

My late husband, Ed, and my foster child Perry Mason (not the one in the wheelchair!) couldn't get enough of this liver-and-onions dish.

1 lb calves liver
1 cup all-purpose flour
2 eggs
2 cups dry breadcrumbs
2 tbsp lard
4 onions, sliced

Pour hot water over liver and let stand for 10 minutes. Remove from water and lightly pat dry. Put the flour in a pie plate. In a second pie plate, beat the eggs well. Put the breadcrumbs in another pie plate. Press both sides of the liver into the flour; dip into the eggs and then into breadcrumbs. In a frying pan over medium heat, melt some shortening or lard. Brown liver for 5 minutes on both sides or until done; don't overcook. Meanwhile, in another frying pan, cook the onions until translucent. Cover the liver with the onions and serve with mashed potatoes and vegetables.

Substitution: You can replace the onions with bacon, or you can have both.

Ed and Perry Mason (their birthdays were on the same day).

Liver with Rice

SERVES 5 TO 6

This is a different way of doing liver!

5 slices bacon
1-1/2 lb calves liver
1 onion, sliced
1 green pepper, sliced into strips
1/4 tsp chili powder
Pinch of garlic powder
1/2 pouch tomato vegetable soup mix
1/3 cup water
5–6 cups cooked rice

In a frying pan, fry bacon until crisp; drain, reserving bacon fat. Crumble bacon and set aside. Cut liver into bite-size pieces. In 3 tbsp of bacon fat, sauté the liver, onion, green pepper, chili powder and garlic powder until liver is brown. Stir in soup mix, water and bacon. Simmer, covered, for 10 minutes or until liver is tender, stirring often. Serve on a bed of cooked rice.

Helen's Chops

Overleaf: Mother and child; in the 1960s.

Breaded Pork Chops with Cheese

SERVES 6

My family and friends love this recipe so much I have to double it every time I make it.

6 pork chops
2 eggs
1-1/2 cups fine dry breadcrumbs
3/4 cup grated Parmesan cheese
1 tsp salt
1/2 tsp white pepper
1 tsp salt
1/4 tsp garlic powder
1/4 tsp dried basil

Wash and pat dry pork chops. In a pie plate, lightly beat the eggs. In a medium bowl, mix together breadcrumbs, Parmesan, salt, pepper, garlic powder and basil. Dip the pork chops in the eggs and then into the breadcrumb mixture, coating well on both sides. Place coated pork chops in a well-greased baking dish and bake at 350°F for approximately 1 hour or until the pork shows no pink inside. Serve hot.

Pork Chops with Peppers and Rice

SERVES 4

I often make this recipe for my dear friends and neighbours.

4 pork chops, 1-1/2-inches thick
2 tbsp lard
1 clove garlic, chopped
Salt and pepper
1 onion, chopped
2 tbsp chopped red pepper
2 tbsp chopped green pepper
1/2 cup rice
3 cups tomato juice

Wash and dry pork chops. In a frying pan heat lard and add garlic and pork chops; sprinkle with salt and pepper. Cook for 10 minutes or until brown on both sides. Transfer to a deep casserole dish and add onion, peppers, 1/2 tsp salt, rice and tomato juice. Bake, covered, at 350°F for approximately 1 hour or until the rice is soft and the pork chops are completely cooked.

Pork Chop Casserole with Peppers, Carrots and Peas

SERVES 6

This is one of my favourite Sunday-dinner recipes: it's fast, easy and—most important—tasty!

1 cup rice
6 pork chops
2 cloves garlic, chopped fine
1 large onion, chopped
1/2 green pepper, chopped
1/2 red pepper, chopped
1 10-oz can cream of mushroom soup
1 cup water
1 tsp salt
1/2 tsp white pepper
1/4 tsp dried basil
1 cup frozen mixed peas and carrots

Boil rice in 2 cups salted water until half-cooked; drain and return to pan. Wash and pat dry pork chops. Brown pork chops in a frying pan with garlic for 10 minutes. Remove pork chops and set aside. In the same pan, sauté the onion and peppers until onion is translucent. Remove from heat. Add to the half-cooked rice the soup, water, salt, pepper, basil, peas and carrots and the cooked onions and peppers. Spoon half of the rice mixture into a well-greased baking dish. Top with 3 of the browned pork chops, then the remaining rice, and then the remaining pork chops. Bake, covered, at 350°F for 1 hour or until the rice is soft and the pork chops are well done.

Frank's Favourite Fried Pork Chops with Fried Apples

SERVES 4 TO 6

Although I'm a Winnipegger, I was born and bred as a Saskatchewan girl. My father the farmer, Frank (who raised four kids, with help from his sister-in-law), particularly loved this recipe.

6 pork chops
1/2 tsp salt
1/2 tsp pepper
1/2 tsp paprika
1/4 tsp garlic powder
2 tbsp lard
4 apples, cored and sliced 1/4-inch thick

Wash and pat dry pork chops. In a small bowl, mix together salt, pepper, paprika and garlic powder. Sprinkle the mixture on the pork chops. In a frying pan, heat the lard. Brown pork chops on both sides for 10 minutes. Reduce heat and cook slowly until tender. Remove pork chops and keep warm. Add apples to pan and fry until tender, 4 to 5 minutes, stirring often to make sure they don't burn. Serve apples over the pork chops.

Roasted Pork Chops with Tomatoes and Basil

SERVES 2 TO 4

The simplicity of this dish means I always have more time to watch Kenny and the "big girl."

1 tbsp vegetable oil
4 pork chops
2 cloves garlic, minced
1 onion, chopped
2 tsp dried basil
1/2 tsp salt
1/2 tsp pepper
3 tomatoes, chopped
3 potatoes, chopped

In a large frying pan, heat oil; cook pork chops with garlic and half of the onion until chops are browned on both sides, approximately 10 minutes. Transfer the pork chops to a baking dish and add the rest of the onion, basil, salt, pepper and tomatoes. Arrange the potatoes around the pork chops. Bake, uncovered, at 375°F for approximately 25 minutes or until pork shows no pink inside and vegetables are tender.

Pork Loin Roast with Garlic

SERVES 2 TO 3

I love this pork dish—it's hearty and tastes great.

3 lb pork loin roast
8–10 cloves garlic, chopped
1 small onion, cut into quarters
2 carrots, chopped
2 potatoes, cubed
1 tsp dried basil
1 tsp dried oregano
1/2 tsp salt
1/2 tsp pepper
1/2 cup beef stock

Place the roast in a baking dish. Arrange the garlic, onion, carrots and potatoes around the roast. Sprinkle with the basil, oregano, salt and pepper. Add the stock and bake, uncovered, at 400°F for approximately 30 minutes or until the vegetables are tender and the roast shows no pink inside.

Roasted Ham Steaks with Apple and Cinnamon

SERVES 4

My late husband, Ed—the best man I've ever known—really enjoyed this roasted ham dish.

1/2 cup apple juice
2 tbsp brown sugar
3/4–1 tsp cinnamon
1 tsp paprika
1 tsp garlic powder
1 tsp parsley flakes
4 ham steaks, 1/2-inch thick
3 large apples, cored and cut into quarters

In a baking dish large enough to hold the ham steaks, mix together apple juice, brown sugar, cinnamon, paprika, garlic powder and parsley. Place the ham in the mixture and let sit for about 10 minutes. Place the apple pieces around the ham and bake at 375°F for 5 minutes, basting frequently.

The love of my life.

Stir-fried Pork with Honey and Garlic

SERVES 4

This is one of the dishes that always has them screaming for more.

4 boneless pork loin chops
2 tbsp vegetable oil
4 cloves garlic, minced
1 cup sliced onions
2 large carrots, sliced thin
1 green pepper, sliced
1 cup broccoli florets
1 small zucchini, chopped
1/2 cup soy sauce
1/4 cup liquid honey

Cut the pork chops into strips. In a large frying pan, heat the oil with garlic and add the pork strips. Stir-fry until they're no longer pink inside, approximately 4 to 5 minutes. Add onions and stir-fry until translucent. Add carrots, green pepper, broccoli and zucchini; stir-fry for another 3 to 4 minutes. Add soy sauce and honey; stir-fry for 2 minutes more. Serve immediately.

Chili with Ground Pork

SERVES 6

I actually got along with my in-laws—probably because whenever they visited, I served them the following recipe.

2 tbsp vegetable oil
1-1/2 lb ground pork
2 cloves garlic, minced
1 small onion, chopped
1 green pepper, chopped
2 carrots, chopped
1/2 cup chopped celery
1 28-oz can stewed tomatoes
1 19-oz can red kidney beans, rinsed
2 tbsp chili powder
1/2 tsp dried basil
1/2 tsp salt
1/2 tsp pepper

Heat oil in a large saucepan and brown the ground pork. Make a well in the centre and add garlic, onion, green pepper, carrots and celery; sauté until the onion is translucent. Stir in tomatoes, kidney beans, chili powder, basil, salt and pepper. Simmer, uncovered, stirring occasionally, for 20 to 25 minutes. Serve hot.

The late Grandma Kostick, in Winnipeg.

Pork Sausage with Green Peas, Onions and Mashed Potatoes

SERVES 2

My brother Alfred loved this dish.

1-1/2 lb pork sausages
1 tbsp lard
1 clove garlic, minced
1-1/2 tbsp flour
1 cup water
2 onions, sliced thin
1 cup frozen peas
Pinch of salt
Pinch of pepper
3 cups (approx.) mashed potatoes

In a large frying pan, brown the sausages in lard and garlic. Transfer sausages to a buttered baking dish. Add the flour to the pan, and cook, stirring, for 2 minutes. Mix in the water, bring to a slow boil and cook, stirring, until gravy is thickened. Layer the onions over the sausages and sprinkle with the peas; sprinkle with salt and pepper. Pour gravy over peas then top with the mashed potatoes. Bake at 350°F for 30 to 45 minutes or until the mashed potatoes are golden brown. Serve hot.

Don't Forget the Lamb!

Overleaf: Me and my favourite sister, Phyllis.

Lamb Chops with Baked Apples

SERVES 6 TO 8

The apples give these lamb chops a wonderful taste.

3/4 cup apple juice
1/2 cup applesauce
1 tbsp lemon juice
1 small onion, chopped fine
2 cloves garlic, crushed
1/2 tsp dried basil
Pinch of salt
1/2 tsp pepper
1 tbsp olive oil
8 lamb chops, about 1-1/2–2 inches thick
4 apples, cored and quartered

In a shallow baking dish, combine apple juice, applesauce, lemon juice, onion, garlic, basil, salt and pepper.

In a frying pan, heat the olive oil and brown the lamb chops on both sides.

Place chops in baking dish; arrange apple quarter pieces around the chops. Bake at 350°F for 30 to 40 minutes or until the chops are completely cooked.

Lamb Chops with Green Pepper

SERVES 4

When you're done cooking, you'll have plenty of "sauce" left. Serve it over the chops—it's delicious.

4 lamb chops
2 tbsp vegetable oil
1 cup beef stock
2 carrots, sliced
2 green peppers, sliced
1 tsp dried basil
1 28-oz can stewed tomatoes, chopped
1/2 tsp salt
1/2 tsp pepper

In a large frying pan, sauté the lamb chops in oil for 2 to 4 minutes on each side. Remove and set aside.

In the same pan, heat the stock. Add the carrots, green peppers and basil; simmer for 5 minutes. Return the chops to the pan and add tomatoes; cook for another 8 to 12 minutes or until the chops are thoroughly cooked. Season with salt and pepper and serve chops with sauce on top.

I'm Wonton More: Stir-fries and Other Delights

Overleaf: Ken and an early dance partner.

Deep-Fried Wontons

SERVES 6 TO 8

My good friend and neighbour Mrs. Kwong has many uses for wontons; this is one very good one.

3/4 lb ground pork
8 water chestnuts, chopped
2 stalks green onion, chopped
3 tsp cornstarch
2 tbsp soy sauce
1 tbsp oyster sauce
1 tsp cooking wine
1/2 tsp salt
1/2 tsp pepper
8–10 tiger shrimp, cut into small pieces (optional)
1 16-oz pkg wonton wraps
3 cups oil

In a medium bowl, combine the ground pork, water chestnuts, green onions, cornstarch, soy sauce, oyster sauce, cooking wine, salt, pepper and shrimp (if using); mix well.

Prepare wonton wraps by laying each one on a flat surface. Add 1 tsp of the mixture to centre of wrap. Pick up the corners of each wrap and pinch together.

In a large nonstick frying pan or wok, heat oil until hot but not smoking on medium heat. Add wontons, a few at at time. Fry for approximately 6 to 8 minutes or until wonton is lightly browned. Drain and serve with Sweet-and-Sour Sauce (see page 134).

Wonton Soup

SERVES 6 TO 8

Mrs. Kwong's home-made wonton soup is easier than you'd expect.

3/4 lb ground pork
8 water chestnuts, chopped
2 stalks green onion, chopped
3 tsp cornstarch
2 tbsp soy sauce
1 tbsp oyster sauce
1 tsp cooking wine
1/2 tsp salt
1/2 tsp pepper
8–10 tiger shrimp, cut into small pieces (optional)
1 16-oz pkg wonton wraps
Pork stock or vegetable stock

In a medium bowl, combine the ground pork, water chestnuts, green onions, cornstarch, soy sauce, oyster sauce, cooking wine, salt, pepper and shrimp (if using); mix well.

Prepare wonton wraps by laying on each one on a flat surface. Add 1 tsp of the mixture to centre of wrap. Pick up the corners of each wrap and pinch together.

Fill a large pot 3/4 full of water and bring to a boil; add approximately 15 to 20 wontons at a time. Be careful not to put too many in the pot at one time. Continue boiling until wontons float to the surface; remove from pot, drain and place in individual serving bowls.

In another pot, bring the pork stock to a boil; pour over wontons in each bowl. Garnish with chopped green onions or cilantro and serve.

Lemon Chicken

SERVES 4 TO 6

Here's a tasty variation to your chicken dinner, thanks to the venerable Mrs. Kwong.

4 cups skinless, boneless chicken, cubed
1/2 tsp pepper
1/2 tsp salt
2 tsp cornstarch
1 egg
2 cups fine breadcrumbs
2-1/2 cups oil

LEMON SAUCE:
1 cup water
1/2 cup lemon juice
1/3 cup sugar
1 tbsp vinegar
2 tsp cornstarch mixed with a little water

In a medium bowl, combine chicken, pepper, salt and cornstarch.

In a separate bowl, beat the egg; stir into chicken mixture.

Pour breadcrumbs into a large, shallow bowl. Add the chicken to bowl, mixing to coat evenly on all sides; set aside.

In a large nonstick frying pan or wok, heat oil until hot but not smoking on medium heat. Add breaded chicken pieces in batches to the frying pan, cooking each batch for 6 to 10 minutes or until golden brown. (To check if cooked, take one piece out and cut in half. If there is no pink, chicken is done.) Remove chicken from pot; drain and set aside.

LEMON SAUCE:
In a small pot, combine the water, lemon juice, sugar and vinegar; cook on medium heat, stirring constantly until liquid begins to bubble. Add cornstarch mixture to thicken the sauce. Pour over chicken or into a dish for dipping. Serve with steamed rice.

Chicken Fried Rice

SERVES 4 TO 6

This is another one of Mrs. Kwong's specialties.

2 eggs
2 tbsp oil
1/2 lb chicken, cut into 2- x 1/4-inch strips
1 cup frozen peas
1/4 cup soy sauce
3/4 tsp salt
3/4 tsp pepper
1 tsp sugar
10–12 cups cooked rice
3 stalks green onion, choppped

In a small bowl, beat the eggs; set aside.

In a large nonstick frying pan or wok, heat the oil until hot but not smoking over medium heat. Add the beaten eggs and cook like an omelet. Remove omelet from frying pan or wok and cut into strips.

In the same frying pan or wok, heat 2 tbsp oil until hot but not smoking over medium heat. Add chicken and stir-fry until no longer pink, about 1 minute. Add the peas, soy sauce, salt, pepper and sugar and stir well. Mix in cooked rice, egg strips and green onions, stir-frying for another minute; add salt and pepper to taste.

Serve hot with vegetables.

Stir-fried Chinese Greens with Beef

SERVES 4 TO 6

Although this recipe calls for bok choy, a type of Chinese cabbage that you can find in your local supermarket, Mrs. Kwong often uses other Chinese vegetables such as gai-lan or yu-coy (you'll likely have to check out the local Chinese food market for these).

Leaves from 1 head of bok choy
2 tbsp soy sauce
1-1/2 tbsp oyster sauce
2 tbsp cooking wine
2 tsp sugar
1/2 tsp salt
2 tbsp oil
2 cloves garlic, finely chopped
3/4 lb beef, cut into 2- x 1/4-inch strips
2 tsp cornstarch mixed with 4 tsp water

In a steamer, steam the bok choy leaves until tender; set aside.

Meanwhile, in a small bowl, combine the soy sauce, oyster sauce, wine, sugar and salt; set aside.

In a large nonstick frying pan or wok, heat the oil until hot but not smoking over medium heat. Add the garlic and stir-fry for 1 minute. Add the beef and stir-fry until the beef is no longer pink, about 1 minute. Add the soy sauce mixture and bok choy and bring to a boil. Stir in the cornstarch mixture and cook, stirring constantly, until slightly thickened, about 1 minute. Serve hot with steamed rice.

Beef Fried Rice

SERVES 6 TO 8

This is an oh-so-slight variation on Mrs. Kwong's Chicken Fried Rice.

2 eggs
2 tbsp oil
1/2 lb beef, cut into 2- x 1/4-inch strips
1 cup frozen peas
1/4 cup soy sauce
3/4 tsp salt
3/4 tsp pepper
1 tsp sugar
10 cups cooked rice
3 stalks green onion, chopped

In a small bowl, beat the eggs; set aside.

In a large nonstick frying pan or wok, heat the oil until hot but not smoking over medium heat. Add the beaten eggs and cook like an omelet. Remove omelet from frying pan or wok and cut into strips.

In the same frying pan or wok, heat another 2 tbsp oil until hot but not smoking over medium heat. Add beef and stir-fry until no longer pink, about 1 minute. Add the peas, soy sauce, salt, pepper and sugar and stir well. Mix in cooked rice, egg strips and green onions, stir-frying for another minute; add salt and pepper to taste. Serve hot with vegetables.

Substitution: If you don't have beef or chicken, try stir-frying pork or shrimp.

Beef with Stewed Tomatoes

SERVES 4 TO 6

And what, you ask, is exotic about this? Well, it's all in the method; just add soy sauce and sugar and stir-fry up a feast.

2 tbsp oil
1 clove garlic, finely chopped
3/4 lb beef, cut into strips
2 tbsp soy sauce
2 tbsp sugar
1 medium onion, sliced
1 cup canned stewed tomatoes
2 tsp cornstarch mixed with 4 tsp water

In a large nonstick frying pan or wok, heat the oil until hot but not smoking on medium heat. Add the garlic and stir-fry for 1 minute. Add the beef and stir-fry until beef is no longer pink, about 1 minute. Add the soy sauce, sugar and onion, stirring for 2 minutes. Add the stewed tomatoes and stir-fry for another 3 minutes. Stir in the cornstarch mixture to thicken; continue stirring for 1 minute more. Serve hot with steamed rice.

Breaded Sweet-and-Sour Pork with Pineapple

SERVES 6

I'm not sure if pineapples grow in China, or anywhere west of Hawaii, but they sure tart up this sweet-and-sour number—compliments go to Mrs. Kwong, naturally.

1-1/2 to 2 lb pork, cubed
1 tsp pepper
1/2 tsp salt
2 tsp cornstarch
1 egg
2 cups fine bread crumbs
3 cups oil

SWEET-AND-SOUR SAUCE:
1 cup water
1/2 cup vinegar
1/3 cup sugar
1/4 cup ketchup
2–3 rings pineapple, cut into small pieces
2 tsp cornstarch mixed with 4 tsp water

In a large bowl, combine pork, pepper, salt and cornstarch.

In a separate bowl, beat the egg and add to pork mixture.

Pour breadcrumbs into a large, shallow bowl. Roll the pork pieces, a few at a time, in the breadcrumbs, making sure all sides are evenly coated; set aside.

In a large nonstick frying pan or wok, heat the oil until hot but not smoking on medium heat. Add the breaded pork pieces, several at a time, cooking each batch for 10 to 12 minutes or until golden brown. (To ensure it is cooked, cut one breaded pork cube in half and if no longer pink in the centre, pork is done.)

Sweet-and-Sour Sauce:
In a small pot, combine the water, vinegar, sugar, ketchup and pineapple. Cook on medium-high heat, stirring constantly, until liquid starts to bubble. Add the cornstarch mixture, stirring to thicken. Pour over top of breaded pork or in a bowl, for dipping. Serve with streamed rice.

Substitution: There's absolutely no substitution for this!

Me and Ken with my nephews Larry, Kelvin and Doug—quite a few years ago.

Stir-fried Pork with Bean Sprouts

SERVES 4 TO 6

I've saved the pork for last: this is definitely one of Mrs. Kwong's tastiest dishes.

2 tbsp oil
2 cloves garlic, chopped
1/2 lb pork, cut into thin slices
1 medium onion, sliced
2 tbsp oyster sauce
1/2 tsp salt
3–4 slices fresh ginger (optional)
1-1/2 lb bean sprouts
2 tsp cornstarch mixed with 4 tsp water

In a large nonstick frying pan or wok, heat the oil until hot but not smoking on medium heat. Add the garlic and stir-fry for 1 minute. Add the pork and stir-fry until pork is no longer pink in the centre, about 3 to 4 minutes. Add the onion, oyster sauce, salt and ginger slices if using, stirring for 2 minutes. Add the bean sprouts and stir-fry for another 2 minutes or until bean sprouts are translucent. Make a well in the centre and add cornstarch mixture to thicken; continue stirring for 1 minute more. Serve hot with steamed rice.

Substitution: Replace the pork with any kind of meat you want; or don't even bother adding meat. I suppose you could try tofu (not exactly a favourite of mine. It is, however, something Kenny would do).

continued from p. 137

Overleaf: Three cheeky monkeys.

Lay It On Me: Baked Goods

continued on page 138

Peanut Butter Cookies

MAKES 60 SMALL COOKIES

These have always been Ken's favourite cookies.

1 cup butter, softened
1-1/4 cups smooth peanut butter
1 cup white sugar
1 cup brown sugar
2 large eggs
2 tsp vanilla extract
3 cups all-purpose flour
2 tsp baking soda

In a large bowl, cream the butter; mix in peanut butter. Add white and brown sugar and continue mixing. Add the eggs and vanilla and mix using a wooden spoon. Then mix in flour and baking soda. The dough should be soft.

Form a teaspoonful at a time into a ball and place on an ungreased cookie sheet. Press a floured fork across the middle of each to flatten slightly. Bake at 375°F for 15 minutes or until lightly browned.

Substitution: Use crunchy peanut butter if you want.

Oatmeal Orange Cookies with Coconut

MAKES 30 COOKIES

Ken's friend and next-door neighbour Gill can't get enough of these.

1 cup all-purpose flour
1 cup sugar
2 tsp baking powder
1/2 tsp salt
1/2 tsp nutmeg
1/2 cup shortening
1 egg
Zest of 1 orange
2 tbsp orange juice
1-1/2 cups quick-cooking rolled oats
1 cup unsweetened flaked coconut

Sift flour, sugar, baking powder, salt and nutmeg into a medium bowl. Add shortening, egg, orange zest and juice; beat until smooth and well blended. Mix in the rolled oats and coconut. Drop dough by teaspoonfuls about 3 inches apart on greased cookie sheet. Cook at 375°F for 12 to 15 minutes, until edges are lightly browned.

Substitution: You can replace coconut with 1/2 cup crushed almonds.

Boiled-Raisin Drop Cookies

MAKES 6 DOZEN COOKIES

At Christmas I always add mixed fruit.

2 cups raisins
1 cup water
1 tsp baking soda
4 cups all-purpose flour
1 tsp baking powder
1 cup shortening
2 tsp salt
1-1/2 tsp cinnamon
1/4 tsp nutmeg
1/4 tsp allspice
Pinch of ground cloves
2 cups sugar
3 large eggs, well beaten
1 tsp vanilla extract
1 cup chopped walnuts

In a small pot, boil the raisins in water for 5 minutes; remove from heat and let cool (do not drain). Stir in the baking soda.

Sift flour with baking powder. In a bowl, blend shortening with salt and spices. Slowly add sugar, mixing thoroughly. Add eggs, vanilla, raisins and their liquid, and flour mixture; mix well. Stir in nuts. Chill dough until stiff.

Drop by rounded teaspoonfuls onto a greased cookie sheet and bake at 400°F for 10 to 12 minutes or until cookies are golden brown.

No-Bake Coconut Chocolate Drops

MAKES 2 DOZEN

Drops are very easy to make—and everyone enjoys them.

2 cups sugar
1/2 cup margarine
1/2 cup milk
3 cups quick-cooking rolled oats
1-1/2 cups unsweetened shredded coconut
1/3 cup cocoa
1/2 tsp vanilla extract
1/4 tsp salt

In a saucepan, boil the sugar, margarine and milk for 1 minute. Remove from heat and stir in the oats, coconut, cocoa, vanilla and salt. Stir well and drop by teaspoonfuls onto waxed paper. Let cool.

Will Ken ever forgive me for this? (see also page 159)

Chocolate Chip Cookies

MAKES 60 COOKIES

These cookies are almost everyone's favourite but especially Constables Andrew Tighe and Robert Cox and unconstable Donald Martin.

1-1/2 cups shortening
2-1/2 cups brown sugar
2 eggs
1/4 cup milk
1 tbsp vanilla extract
3 cups all-purpose flour
2 tsp salt
1-1/2 tsp baking soda
3 cups semisweet chocolate chips

In a large bowl, blend shortening and sugar with an electric mixer for 2 to 3 minutes. Add eggs, milk and vanilla; beat for 2 minutes. Add flour, salt and baking soda; beat on low speed for 1 to 2 minutes, until well blended. Stir in chocolate chips.

Drop by teaspoonfuls 1-1/2 inches apart on an ungreased baking sheet. Bake at 375°F for 10 to 12 minutes. Let cool and remove onto a paper towel.

Shortbread Cookies (no. 1)

MAKES 30 SMALL COOKIES

I make these at Christmas time with small pieces of green and red candied cherries pressed into the centre. All the neighbourhood children love them.

1 cup butter, softened
1/2 cup icing sugar
1-1/2 cups all-purpose flour

Cream butter and icing sugar until smooth; stir in the flour until doughy. Roll a small piece of dough for each cookie and place on an ungreased cookie sheet. With your finger, press a small dimple in the middle, or press a small piece of red or green candied cherry in the middle.

Bake at 350°F for 10 to 12 minutes or until edges are lightly browned.

Substitution: You can use margarine instead of butter, but your cookies will taste different.

Shortbread Cookies (no. 2)

MAKES 60 SMALL COOKIES

My foster children loved these at Christmas time.

1-1/4 lb butter, softened
1-1/4 cups fruit sugar
4-1/4 cups all-purpose flour

In a large bowl, cream the butter and sugar together. Slowly mix in the flour, a little at a time. On a clean work surface, knead dough well. Roll out 1/4-inch thick, cut into any shape you want and bake cookies on an ungreased cookie sheet at 350°F for approximately 15 minutes or until edges are golden brown.

Substitution: You can add mixed fruit to these cookies.

Shortbread (no. 3)

MAKES 60 COOKIES

I like to give pastries as gifts to those who don't have the time to bake. That's why I have so many shortbread recipes!

1 lb unsalted butter, softened
4-1/3 cups all-purpose flour
1 cup cornstarch
1 cup icing sugar

Cream butter well. Add the flour; mix well. Add cornstarch and icing sugar; mix again. Let stand for 1 hour. On a very lightly floured work surface, roll out dough and cut or shape the way you want. Place on an ungreased cookie sheet and bake at 350°F for 15 to 20 minutes or until the edges are lightly browned.

Walnut Squares

MAKES 12 SQUARES

This is a very nice square to make for showers or parties.

PASTRY:
1-1/2 cups all-purpose flour
1/4 cup brown sugar
1/2 cup cold butter

MERINGUE TOPPING:
2 egg whites
1 cup brown sugar
2 tbsp all-purpose flour
1/2 tsp baking powder
1 cup chopped walnuts
1/2 cup sweetened shredded coconut

PASTRY:
In a large bowl, combine pastry ingredients until mixture becomes crumbly. Press into a greased, shallow 7- x 11-inch cake pan. Bake at 350°F for 10 minutes or until brown. Let cool.

MERINGUE TOPPING:
In a medium bowl, beat the egg whites until stiff. Gradually beat in sugar, beating well after each addition. Blend in flour and baking powder. Fold in nuts and coconuts.

Spread mixture evenly over cooled pastry. Bake at 325°F until meringue is light brown, approximately 15 to 20 minutes. While still warm, cut into squares and let cool in pan.

Bran Muffins

MAKES 36 MUFFINS

These muffins are a big hit with a lot of people. I used to regularly ship a batch to my father in Saskatchewan. Today, members of the Winnipeg Police Department often drop by for a muffin or two.

5 cups all-bran cereal
2 cups sugar
1 cup vegetable oil
1 cup warm water
1 cup raisins or dates
3 eggs
3 cups milk
3 cups all-purpose flour
2-1/2 tsp baking soda
1/4 tsp salt

In a large bowl combine all-bran, sugar, oil, water, raisins, eggs and milk; mix with a wooden spoon. Add flour, baking soda and salt; mix well. Let stand for 10 minutes so the cereal will become soft. Mix again. Fill muffin tins 1/2 full and bake at 350°F for 30 minutes or until browned.

Blueberry Muffins

MAKES 12 MUFFINS

These are wonderful fresh, for breakfast or brunch.

2 cups all-purpose flour
2 tsp baking powder
1/2 tsp salt
1/4 cup sugar
2 cups blueberries
1 egg, beaten
3/4 cup milk
1/4 cup soft shortening

In a medium bowl, sift together flour, baking powder, salt and sugar; stir in the berries.

In a separate bowl, combine egg, milk and shortening. Add to dry ingredients, stirring to blend well. Fill greased muffin tins 2/3 full and bake at 400°F for approximately 20 minutes or until browned.

Apple Crisp

SERVES 6 TO 8

Apple Crisp is a great, hearty dessert most everyone will like, especially with ice cream.

5 cups sliced apples
1-1/2 tbsp lemon juice
2 tbsp brown sugar
1/2 cup water

TOPPING:
1-1/2 cups quick-cooking rolled oats
3/4 cup packed brown sugar
1/2 cup all-purpose flour
1-1/4 tsp cinnamon
1/2 tsp salt
1/2 cup melted butter

Place sliced apples in a greased 9-inch square baking dish; sprinkle with lemon juice, brown sugar and water. Mix together all the topping ingredients until crumbly. Sprinkle over apples. Bake at 375°F for 30 to 35 minutes or until apples are soft. Serve hot, warm or cold.

Rhubarb Crisp

SERVES 6

My Rhubarb Crisp recipe works best when the rhubarb is "young." It tastes great with ice cream.

1 cup quick-cooking rolled oats
6 tbsp brown sugar
1/4 cup all-purpose flour
2 tbsp cold butter
4 cups chopped rhubarb
1/2 cup white sugar

In a medium bowl, combine oats, brown sugar and flour. Cut or rub in butter until it becomes crumbly. In a separate bowl, stir together well the rhubarb and white sugar.

In a 5- x 9-inch casserole dish, spread half of the crumb mixture. Top with the rhubarb, then top with the remaining crumbs. Bake at 350°F for 50 to 60 minutes or until the top is golden brown.

Apple Cinnamon Roll-ups

MAKES 60 ROLL-UPS

These roll-ups are great lunchbox goodies.

5-1/2 cups all-purpose flour
2-1/4 tsp baking powder
1/2 tsp salt
1 lb margarine
2 eggs, beaten
1 cup milk
2 cups sugar
2-1/2 tbsp cinnamon
1 cup apple pie filling, crushed

In a large bowl, stir together flour, baking powder and salt. Cut in margarine until mixture is like coarse meal. Add eggs and milk; stir until mixture forms a dough. Divide dough into 8 to 10 balls and chill, uncovered, in the fridge 8 hours or overnight.

Mix sugar and cinnamon; spread over countertop. Roll out each ball of dough over the cinnamon and sugar; it should be the size of piecrust. Cut into wedges, spread each wedge with 1/2 tsp apple filling and roll up, starting from the wide end. Arrange on an ungreased cookie sheet and bake at 375°F until lightly browned.

Banana Coconut Loaf

MAKES 1 LOAF

This is a great loaf to try when you have too many ripe or overripe bananas.

2-1/2 cups sifted all-purpose flour
1 tbsp baking powder
1 tsp salt
1 tsp cinnamon
1/2 tsp nutmeg
1/4 tsp baking soda
1/2 cup shortening
1 cup sugar
3 eggs
1 tsp vanilla extract
1-1/4 cups mashed ripe bananas (about 2 large)
1 cup unsweetened shredded coconut

Sift together flour, baking powder, salt, cinnamon, nutmeg and baking soda. In a medium bowl, cream shortening until soft. Gradually add sugar, creaming after each addition. Add eggs one at a time, beating well after each one. Stir in vanilla. Add flour mixture a little at a time, alternating with the mashed bananas. Blend until smooth after each addition. Stir in coconut. Turn into a greased 6- x 9-inch loaf pan. Bake at 350°F for 35 to 40 minutes or until a tester comes out clean.

Date and Orange Nut Loaf

MAKES 1 LOAF

I make several of these loaves at one time and freeze them—they make a great change from biscuits to serve with tea and coffee.

1 large orange
3/4 cup boiling water
2 cups all-purpose flour
1/2 cup sugar
2 tsp baking powder
1/2 tsp baking soda
1/4 tsp salt
2 tbsp melted butter
1 tsp vanilla extract
1 cup chopped dates
1/2 cup chopped walnuts

Wash orange; extract juice and chop rind very fine. In a small bowl, pour boiling water over rind and juice.

In a medium bowl, sift together flour, sugar, baking powder, baking soda and salt. Pour in orange mixture, melted butter, vanilla, dates and nuts; mix well. Pour into a well-greased 5- x 8-inch loaf pan. Let stand for 25 minutes. Bake at 350°F for 1 hour or until lightly browned. Let cool in pan before slicing.

Butter Slice

MAKES ONE 8-INCH SQUARE CAKE

Butter Slice never lasted very long with my family—I loved watching them devour it.

BOTTOM:
1/2 cup cold butter
1 cup all-purpose flour
2 tbsp brown sugar

TOPPING:
2 eggs
1-1/2 cups brown sugar
1/4 cup melted butter
2 tbsp white vinegar
1 tsp vanilla extract
1 cup currants or raisins
1/2 cup chopped walnuts (optional)

In a bowl, combine the bottom ingredients until crumbly. Pat the mixture into an 8-inch square cake pan. For the topping, in a bowl, beat the eggs. Beat in the sugar, melted butter, vinegar and vanilla. Stir in the currants and walnuts (if using). Spread mixture in pan. Bake at 350°F for 40 minutes or until lightly browned on top.

Apricot Slices

MAKES 12

You really don't need a special occasion or event to make these slices because it's great any time.

BOTTOM:
1-1/2 cups all-purpose flour
1/2 cup soft butter
1 egg, beaten
1 tbsp milk

FILLING:
3/4 cup apricot jam

TOPPING:
1/4 cup melted butter
3/4 cup sugar
1 egg, beaten
1 cup unsweetened shredded coconut
1 tsp vanilla extract

To make the bottom, in a medium bowl, mix together flour, butter, egg and milk. Line a 10- x 6-inch cake pan with the mixture. Cover with the apricot jam.

To make the topping, in a separate bowl, beat melted butter with sugar, then stir in the egg, coconut and vanilla. Spread over jam. Bake at 350°F for 30 minutes or until the top is lightly browned. Let cool in pan and cut into squares.

Walnut Applesauce Cake

MAKES ONE 8-INCH ROUND CAKE PAN

This was Ken's lunchbox snack.

1 cup sugar
1 tsp cinnamon
1/2 tsp ground cloves
1/4 tsp nutmeg
1/2 cup shortening
1 egg, beaten
1 cup thick unsweetened applesauce
1 tsp vanilla extract
2 cups all-purpose flour
1 tsp baking soda
1 tsp baking powder
1/2 tsp salt
1 cup chopped walnuts
3/4 cup chopped raisins (optional)

In a large bowl, mix together sugar, cinnamon, cloves and nutmeg. Add shortening; cream. Stir in the egg. Stir in applesauce and vanilla. In a separate bowl, sift together flour, baking soda, baking powder and salt; add to shortening mixture and beat well. Add walnuts and raisins (if using). Turn into greased 8-inch layer pan and bake at 350°F for 35 minutes or until toothpick inserted in the centre comes out clean.

Apple Cake with Brown Sugar Sauce

MAKES ONE 8- X 10-INCH CAKE

This is a great dessert for any night of the week. You can also serve the cake with cream.

1-1/2 cups all-purpose flour
1/4 cup sugar
3 tsp baking powder
1/2 tsp salt
3 tbsp shortening
1 egg
2/3 cup milk
3 apples
2 tbsp sugar
Pinch of cinnamon

SAUCE:
3/4 cup brown sugar
1 tsp cornstarch
1/4 tsp salt
1 cup boiling water
1 tsp butter
1/2 tsp vanilla extract

Sift flour, sugar, baking powder and salt into a bowl; cut in shortening with a pastry blender. Beat egg and milk together; pour into the flour mixture; stirring to make a soft dough. Spread in a greased 8- x 10-inch pan. Peel and core apples, then slice into eighths. Press each piece into the dough and sprinkle with sugar and cinnamon. Bake at 375°F for 35 minutes or until toothpick inserted in centre comes out clean.

SAUCE:

In a small saucepan, mix sugar, cornstarch and salt. Over medium heat, slowly add boiling water, stirring until thickened. Remove from heat and stir in butter and vanilla.

Will Ken ever forgive me for this? (see also page 142)

Quick and Easy Blueberry Cake

MAKES ONE 9- x 13-INCH CAKE

I made this cake when Ken was visiting his cottage. When he finished the whole thing he said, "Mom, don't bring any more cake, okay?" Hey, Ken, so much for low-fat!

3 eggs
1 cup sugar
1/2 cup vegetable oil
1 tsp vanilla extract
1-1/2 cups all-purpose flour
2 tsp baking powder
Pinch of salt
2 cups blueberry pie filling

Using an electric mixer, in a medium bowl, beat the eggs, sugar, oil and vanilla for 3 minutes at high speed. Add the flour, baking powder and salt; beat at low speed until the mixture is smooth. Pour into a greased 9- x 13-inch cake pan and spread out the dough. Spoon the blueberry filling evenly over the dough. Bake at 350°F for 35 to 45 minutes or until a toothpick inserted in the centre comes out clean.

Substitution: Any other pie filling, such as cherry or peach, can be used.

Pineapple Cake

MAKES ONE 9- x 13-INCH CAKE

My nephew Doug MacDougall, who lives in Saskatchewan, can't get enough of this cake.

BOTTOM:
2 cups all-purpose flour
1 cup cold butter
1 cup brown sugar
2 tsp baking powder

FILLING:
2 19-oz cans crushed pineapple
7 tbsp cornstarch
1 cup sugar
2 tsp butter

TOPPING:
2 eggs
1/2 cup sugar
1-1/2 cups unsweetened shredded coconut
2 tsp vanilla extract

To make the bottom, mix all ingredients together with your hands until crumbly. Pack well into a 9- x 13-inch cake pan.

In a saucepan on medium-high heat, cook pineapple, cornstarch and sugar, stirring until mixture thickens. Remove from heat and stir in butter. Let cool, then spread pineapple filling over crumbs.

To make topping, in a medium bowl beat the eggs and sugar together; stir in coconut and vanilla. Spread over the pineapple filling. Bake at 325°F for approximately 45 minutes or until topping is lightly browned.

Crumb Date Cake

MAKES ONE 8-INCH SQUARE CAKE

When I had children going to school, my Crumb Date Cake was very popular for the school teas.

CRUMB MIXTURE:
1-1/2 cups quick-cooking rolled oats
1-1/2 cups all-purpose flour
1 cup brown sugar
3/4 tsp baking powder
3/4 tsp baking soda
3/4 tsp salt
3/4 cup butter or margarine

DATE FILLING:
1 lb chopped dates
3/4 cup water
3 tbsp brown sugar
1 tbsp lemon juice

CRUMB MIXTURE:
Mix together in a large bowl the oats, flour, sugar, baking powder, baking soda and salt. Using your hands, rub the butter into the dry mixture until it becomes like crumbs. Put half the crumb mixture into a greased 8-inch square cake pan; save the other half for top.

DATE FILLING:
In a saucepan, cook dates with water and sugar until soft; let cool. Stir in lemon juice.

Spread filling over the crumb layer and sprinkle with the remaining crumbs; pat lightly. Bake at 350°F for 25 to 30 minutes or until lightly browned. Cool and cut into squares.

Substitution: Instead of dates, make a raisin filling. Just cook everything together the same way, saving the lemon juice for last.

Raisin filling:
2-1/2 cups raisins
1-1/4 cups water
3 tbsp brown sugar
2-1/2 tsp cornstarch
1 tbsp lemon juice

A very cute Ken with some friends.

Delicious Date Cake

MAKES ONE 9- x 13-INCH CAKE

Anyone who has a passion for dates will enjoy this cake.

1-1/2 cups water
1 cup chopped dates
1/2 tsp baking soda
2 eggs
1 cup white sugar
1/2 cup shortening or margarine
1-1/2 cups all-purpose flour
1 tsp baking soda
Pinch of salt
1/2 cup brown sugar
1/2 cup chopped walnuts
1/2 cup semisweet chocolate chips

In a saucepan bring water to a boil. Add dates. Reduce heat to low and simmer until dates are soft. Remove from heat and stir in 1/2 tsp of baking soda. Let cool.

In a medium bowl, beat eggs lightly. Beat in white sugar. Beat in shortening. Stir in flour, remaining 1 tsp soda and salt. Mix in cooled dates. Pour into a greased 9- x 13-inch cake pan. Mix together the brown sugar, nuts and chocolate chips; spread over batter. Bake at 325°F for 1 hour or until a toothpick inserted in centre comes out clean.

Sour Cream Chocolate Cake

MAKES ONE 8-INCH SQUARE CAKE

My chocolate cake with sour cream is the traditional Kostick family birthday cake recipe—enjoy!

2 eggs
1-1/4 cups sugar
1/2 tsp baking soda
1 cup thick sour cream
1/2 tsp vanilla extract
2 squares unsweetened chocolate, melted
2 cups cake-and-pastry flour
2 tsp baking powder
1/4 tsp salt

CHOCOLATE FROSTING:
4 squares unsweetened chocolate
1 cup icing sugar
2 eggs
2 tbsp orange juice

In a medium bowl, lightly beat eggs; using an electric mixer, gradually beat in sugar. In another bowl, sift the baking soda into the sour cream and, using a wooden spoon, stir rapidly until foamy; add to the egg mixture, along with the vanilla. Fold in melted chocolate. Sift in the flour, baking powder and salt; stir until smooth.

Turn into a greased 8-inch square pan and bake at 350°F for 35 to 45 minutes or until toothpick inserted in centre comes out clean.

ICING:
Melt the chocolate in a medium bowl set over hot—but not boiling—water. Beat in sifted icing sugar, alternating with eggs. Add orange juice and continue beating until icing is smooth and thick. Add more icing sugar if necessary.

Puffed Wheat Cake

MAKES ONE 8- X 10-INCH CAKE

It wouldn't be Christmas at our house without Puffed Wheat Cake.

1 cup brown sugar
1/2 cup corn syrup
1/2 cup butter
3 tbsp cocoa
10 large marshmallows
1 tsp vanilla
8 cups puffed wheat cereal

In a saucepan, bring to a boil brown sugar, syrup, butter, cocoa and marshmallows. Boil, stirring constantly, for 4 minutes, then remove from heat and stir in vanilla.

In a large bowl, mix together well the puffed wheat and sugar mixture. Place in a greased 8- x 10-inch cake pan; press down, let cool and then cut into squares.

Substitution: Don't be afraid to use margarine instead of butter.

Carrot Christmas Cake

MAKES 2 LOAVES

The late Mrs. Jennie Besyk gave this recipe to me—trust me, you'll love it!

1-1/2 cups vegetable oil
2 cups brown sugar
2 cups finely grated carrots
4 eggs
1 tsp vanilla extract
2 cups mixed candied fruit
1-1/2–2 cups raisins
1 cup chopped walnuts
3 cups all-purpose flour
1 tbsp baking powder
2 tsp baking soda
2 tsp cinnamon
1 tsp salt
1/2 tsp ground cloves
1/4 tsp nutmeg

Place oil in a large bowl; gradually blend in sugar. Mix in carrots, eggs, vanilla, candied fruit, raisins and nuts. Sift together flour, baking powder, baking soda, cinnamon, salt, cloves and nutmeg; mix flour and carrot mixtures together well. Pour into a well-greased 6- x 10-inch loaf pan. Bake at 350°F for 1 hour or until a toothpick inserted in the centre comes out clean.

Pie Pastry

MAKES ENOUGH FOR THREE 9-INCH DOUBLE-CRUST PIES

I stand by this recipe—it has never failed me.

1 lb all-vegetable shortening
4 cups all-purpose flour
3/4 tsp salt
9 tbsp (approx.) cold water
1-1/4 tsp white vinegar

In a medium bowl, cut shortening into pieces. Add flour and salt; with a knife or pastry blender, cut in shortening until covered with flour. Add the water and vinegar; use your hands to mix everything together. Add more water if necessary so dough holds together. Roll out on lightly floured work surface for pies.

Rhubarb Pie

This pie is very easy to make. I hope you enjoy it.

Pie pastry (see page 168)
2 cups rhubarb
1 egg
1 cup sugar
2 tbsp all-purpose flour

Cut rhubarb in 1/4-inch pieces. In a bowl, beat the egg. Stir in sugar and flour. Stir in rhubarb. Line a 9-inch plate with pastry. Fill with rhubarb and cover with top crust. (If desired, brush the crust with a well-beaten egg and sprinkle with white sugar before baking.)

Bake at 425°F for 15 minutes, then reduce heat to 350°F until the rhubarb is soft and the top crust is golden brown.

Sour Cream Raisin Pie

Although very rich, my Sour Cream Raisin Pie is also very delicious.

Baked 9-inch pie shell
1 cup raisins
1 tsp baking soda
1 cup sour cream
3/4 cup brown sugar
1/2 tsp cinnamon
Pinch of salt
2 eggs, separated
3 tbsp icing sugar

In a pot, bring raisins to a boil in enough hot water to show through the raisins. Stir in baking soda, sour cream, brown sugar, cinnamon, salt and egg yolks; boil, stirring, until the mixture is thick. Pour into the pie shell. Beat egg whites with icing sugar until stiff and shiny. Spread over the pie. Bake at 325°F until the peaks are nice and brown.

Apple Pie

This was my late husband's favourite pie. He even peeled the apples for me.

Pie pastry (see page 168)
8 apples, peeled and sliced thin
1/2–3/4 cup sugar
1/2 tsp cinnamon
1/4 tsp nutmeg (optional)
1 tbsp butter
1 egg, beaten

Line a 9-inch pie plate with pastry. Arrange apples in layers in shell, sprinkling each layer with sugar, cinnamon and nutmeg (if using). Dot with butter and cover with top crust. Make several slits in top crust. Brush with some beaten egg and sprinkle with sugar. Bake at 425°F for 15 minutes; reduce heat to 350°F and bake for another 30 to 35 minutes, or until apples are cooked.

A very cute couple.

Blueberry Pie

I usually make a lot of these pies when the berries are freshly picked—that's when it tastes best.

Pie pastry (see page 168)
3 cups fresh or frozen blueberries
3/4–1 cup sugar
1-1/2 tbsp all-purpose flour
Pinch of salt
1-1/2 tsp butter
1 egg, beaten

Line a 9-inch pie plate with pastry. In a bowl, stir together the blueberries, sugar, flour and salt. Add filling to pie shell. Dot with butter. Cover with top crust and make a slit to allow steam to escape; brush with some beaten egg and sprinkle with sugar. Bake at 425°F for 15 minutes; reduce heat to 350°F and continue baking for 20 to 25 minutes or until crust is golden brown.

Apricot Pie

If you don't favour apple or blueberry pies, ya gotta love this!

Baked 9-inch pie shell

FILLING:
1 cup stewed apricots
3/4 cup brown sugar
3 tbsp cornstarch
Pinch of salt
2 cups boiling water
2 egg yolks, beaten
2 tbsp butter
1 tsp vanilla extract

MERINGUE:
3 egg whites
3 tbsp icing sugar

To make stewed apricots, in a saucepan, boil 1/2 cup water; add pitted apricots and reduce heat to medium. Cook for 7 to 8 minutes or until soft. Put through mincer or food mill.

In a large pot, blend sugar, cornstarch and salt. Add boiling water, stirring constantly; cook, stirring, until thick. Reduce to medium heat and stir in egg yolks and cook, stirring, for another 3 minutes. Remove from heat; stir in butter. Let cool. Stir in vanilla and apricots.

To make meringue, beat egg whites and icing sugar until stiff and shiny.

Pour filling into baked pie shell and top with meringue. Bake at 325°F for 15 to 20 minutes or until lightly browned.

Fresh Strawberry Pie

I make this pie with fresh-picked strawberries. You can use an egg wash for the top crust and sprinkle with sugar.

Pie pastry (see page 168)
4 cups strawberries
1 cup sugar
1/3 cup all-purpose flour
1/2 tsp cinnamon (optional)
4 tsp butter

Line a 9-inch pie plate with pastry. Wash and halve strawberries. In a medium bowl, mix together sugar, flour and cinnamon (if using); add strawberries and stir lightly. Pour into pie plate, dot with butter and cover with top crust. Make a slit in top crust to let steam escape. Bake at 425°F for 15 minutes; reduce heat to 350°F and bake for another 20 minutes.

Quick and Easy Strawberry Pie

This makes for a delicious Sunday-afternoon snack.

2 cups sliced strawberries
Baked 9-inch pie shell
1 pkg (170 g) strawberry Jell-O
1 cup whipped cream
1/2 cup icing sugar
1/2 tsp vanilla extract

Put strawberries in the baked pie shell. Make Jell-O according to instructions on box and let stand until it starts to thicken but before it has set. Pour Jell-O over strawberries; chill.

In a bowl, mix together whipped cream, icing sugar and vanilla; chill. Spread whipped topping over pie.

Where to Find Stuff (Recipe Index)